CAREER REINVENTED

HOW TO BUILD AN INDEPENDENT LIFE BY STARTING YOUR OWN BUSINESS

CAREER REINVENTED

HOW TO BUILD AN INDEPENDENT LIFE BY STARTING YOUR OWN BUSINESS

K. GREGG ELLIOTT

DOWNLOAD A FREE BOOK!

READ THIS FIRST

Just to say thanks for buying my book, I would like to give you the full set of stories about the 10 solopreneurs and small businesses that are cited in *Career, Reinvented*.

Get your copy of

How They Did It: Ten wild rides with successful solopreneurs and small business owners

100% FREE!

TO DOWNLOAD GO TO:

https://mailchi.mp/f7efd7d388f8/how-they-did-it

Disclaimer

The advice and strategies found within may not be suitable for every situation or every person. This work is produced and sold with the understanding that neither the author nor the publisher are held responsible for the results accrued from the advice in this book.

ISBN: 978-1-5136-3740-2

DEDICATION

For Mom and Dad.

Thank you for instilling in me the desire, values, and capability necessary to build an Independent Life.

AND

For Bain and Randa:

You could do this!

TABLE OF CONTENTS

Dedication..ix

Acknowledgments xiii

Introduction.. 1

    Chapter 1 What is an Independent Life? 13

**Part I The Coming Jobageddon:
The Why of Self-Employment............................... 29**

    Chapter 2 America's Corporate Job
    Compact is Over 31

    Chapter 3 Artificial Intelligence:
    Centaur vs. Matrix.. 41

    Chapter 4 Sharing Economy to the Rescue?.... 59

**Part II Building An Independent Life:
The How Of Self-Employment 75**

    Chapter 5 What Does it Take to Go
    Independent? 77

Chapter 6 Making the Mid-Life Career Switch .. 97

Chapter 7 Principles for Success in
Self-employment 117

Chapter 8 Where the Opportunities Are.......... 143

Chapter 9 The Payoff from an
Independent Life 167

Please Consider Leaving A Review...................... 179

About the Author.. 181

Bibliography 183

ACKNOWLEDGMENTS

I would like to acknowledge the ten people who kindly gave of their time to be interviewed and who were willing to share with others their hard-won lessons learned on how to build an Independent Life:

Corey
Dan
Ivan
Maurrean
Melanie & José
Misha
Nigel
Pam
Sophie

Thank you also to the Self-Publishing School and SPS Mastermind community as well as the friends, family, and fellow writers who served as beta readers and helped to launch my book. Above all, thanks to Lise Cartwright, an amazing coach and person.

INTRODUCTION

"Tell me, what is it you plan to do with your one wild and precious life?"

- Mary Oliver, Pulitzer prize-winning poet[1]

Jobageddon—"the end of jobs"—is coming. The rate of change in the world of work is starting to rev up and may soon hit warp speed. Anyone who is not preparing for that is likely to be caught flat-footed or worse, unemployed with fewer and fewer opportunities for earning income. You've probably heard or read articles here and there about what AI (artificial intelligence) is going to do to the job market or about the decline of the corporate job.

This book is going to clarify for you what the experts and analysts are saying about three interacting mega-trends affecting the workplace that, taken to-

---

[1] Oliver, Mary. New and Selected Poems. Boston, MA: Beacon Press, 1992.

gether, make a strong case that your job could be at risk over the next several decades. Then it's going to challenge you to begin considering your own path toward an Independent Life, a path I discovered ten years ago.

Advice for mid-life career switchers

Through my own experience as an "accidental businesswoman" beginning at age 47 and through the experiences of numerous other Independent Lifers I have interviewed, you will learn whether you have the key traits you'll need to successfully work for yourself. You'll learn some essential principles that can guide you toward success in running your business. You will also get practical advice and lessons learned on how to initiate the process of working for yourself—with a particular focus on how to switch careers and go independent in mid-life.

Are you ready to take control by working toward an Independent Life that will help you avoid being caught in the jaws of job place turmoil? And what if you are not a "business type"—can you still build an Independent Life?

I never thought I'd be running my own business, and yet here I am, not only running my business for nearly 10 years but now writing about it. I honestly feel that if I can do it, odds are you can too. One aspect of my business is researching little-known and complicated topics, such as how to communicate about prescribed fire (yes, there is such a thing!) or how to explain the economic values of wildlife habitat.

With over twenty years of research and writing experience and a daughter headed to college, I decided to put my skills to use to understand the world of work that she will be facing when she graduates. I wanted to answer the question, "Am I being realistic to encourage my child to think that the skills and ideas she has could be put to use in creating her own business?"

I discovered that answer is a resounding yes!

That's why I have written this book. I want to offer the knowledge that I and others who are part of the "hidden economy" of the self-employed have gained through our experiences so that you can become the independent, creative, successfully self-employed person you were meant to be.

Get a job or create a job?

Why is it that most of us are raised to aim for "getting a job" rather than creating one? As I began research for this book, I started to take note of all the people I interacted with in my daily life who were self-employed or had their own business: my handyman, dance instructor, masseur, hairdresser, general physician, gynecologist, health insurance broker, my daughter's gym owner, my favorite Mexican restaurant, and some of my very best friends. There was an ecosystem of people living Independent Lives all around me, in plain view, and yet they seemed hidden because the dominant news stories about the economy revolve around "jobs" and working for someone else.

Yet slowly, I was able to rid myself of those blinders, and I saw that a huge number of people are self-employed. It felt a little like Dorothy when she wakes up into the technicolor world of Oz.

Unless you are living an Independent Life already, reading this book will change your perspective just as radically. I promise there are people throughout your life with whom you interact on a daily basis who are running their own businesses, leading an Independent Life. It is not so rare. If they can do it, can't you?

One day, as this transformation in my thinking about the world of work was taking place, I heard someone on the radio asking the very question I had been asking myself. Muhammad Yunus, the 2006 Nobel Peace Prize winner who founded microcredit (very small loans for the poor who have no collateral) in Bangladesh, had just published his book, *A World of Three Zeroes*[2]. Here is what he says about the job model of work:

---

[2] Yunus, Muhammad. *A World of Three Zeroes*. Melbourne | London: Scribe Publications, 2017.

"My position has always been that the world has been giving young people a very wrong kind of model, which is a job-oriented model. People have their education, and the first thing they do is they get out and they look for a job. I think that is a very limited ambition for human beings—to find a slot to fit into. A human being is a creative thing. In our DNA we are go-getters and problem-solvers. But instead we just put people into a small slot in a big machine. I think the world should be an entrepreneurship-oriented world."[3]

Mr. Yunus has stated the thesis of this book, that we can and even *should* aspire to be entrepreneurs, for some or all of our careers. Not just to make money, and not necessarily to make a million bucks, but because we are human and it's in our DNA. We enjoy creating things and being responsible for what we have created. We are most motivated when we care about what we are doing.

Jobageddon vs. The Independent Life

An entrepreneurial mindset is also the only sane response to a world in which mega-trends on the horizon are leading us inexorably toward a "jobageddon" of sorts. It's not that there will be no jobs. There will be

---

[3] Shea, Christopher. "Nobelist Muhammad Yunus: Be A Go-Getter, Not A Job Getter." *NPR.Org* (blog). Accessed March 18, 2018. https://www.npr.org/sections/goatsandsoda/2014/09/23/350640122/nobelist-muhammad-yunus-be-a-go-getter-not-a-job-getter.

loss of some and creation of others—a reshuffling of jobs and required skills on a scale not seen before in the history of the world[4].

With stagnant or declining wages predominant in a workplace where most of us will change jobs an average of 10 to 15 times over the course of our careers[5], it just makes sense to plan for an Independent Life. Does an Independent Life mean you will never work for anyone else? Not at all, although for some of us that could be the case.

There is nothing inherently wrong or bad about working for someone else, especially if you enjoy your work and workplace (for the most part) and are paid fairly. There *is* something inherently scary and at the same time really exhilarating and energizing in working for yourself!

For most of us, working toward an Independent Life means learning how to generate skills, insights, and a useful plan for moving from your 9 to 5 (or in some cases 8 to 9) job to one in which you are your own boss.

---

[4] Manyika, James, Susan Lund, Michael Chui, Jacques Bughin, Jonathan Woetzel, Parul Batra, Ryan Ko, and Saurabh Sanghvi. "Jobs Lost, Jobs Gained," December 2017. https://www.mckinsey.com/global-themes/future-of-organizations-and-work/what-the-future-of-work-will-mean-for-jobs-skills-and-wages.

[5] Doyle, Alison. "How Often Do People Change Jobs?" The Balance. Accessed March 19, 2018. https://www.thebalance.com/how-often-do-people-change-jobs-2060467.

Even if you decide that eventually you want to go back into a revolutionary new job market that has just opened up due to advances in artificial intelligence or a new tech product available on the mass market, you will be working from a position of strength if you are already leading an Independent Life. Why? Because you won't have to *settle.* And because the employers running the companies that employ cutting edge technologies will be impressed by someone with the creativity and industry required to run their own business.

More and more people are moving from the practice of cashing a paycheck to invoicing for a paycheck. The number of freelancers in the US is expected to triple in the next two years and surpass the number of employed workers by 2027.[6]

Some who've gone into freelancing have done so because they were forced to by circumstances: losing a job, losing a home, illness, or other crises. Others have begun freelancing as a "side hustle" to bring in extra money. Still others, like me, have jumped ship from a distasteful job and succeeded in making a very good living as a sole proprietor, freelancer, or business founder.

---

[6] Moulton, Cary, and Dave Cosgrave. "Second Annual Self-Employment Report." Freshbooks cloud accounting, February 21, 2018. https://www.freshbooks.com/_themes/freshbooks/brand-assets/2018selfemploymentreport.pdf.

More frequently, freelancing is a preference rather than a necessity. In 2017, 63 percent said they freelanced by choice, up 10 percentage points from 2014. A major factor driving this trend is that many of us feel our eyes have been opened: we see having a diversity of clients and the freedom to expand our services as more secure than being dependent on any one company's "at will" employment.

Meeting change by making the change

If forces are warping the way you will be able to work in the future, making corporate employment more difficult and less plentiful while making freelancing and self-employment easier, why not embrace and plan for change? Rather than waiting for the ax to fall or the AI to hit or whatever other force is going to rock your industry, instead of being forced into finding another way to make ends meet, why not plan now—not only for your future livelihood, but for your Independent Life?

Career, Reinvented will help you do just that, both by providing inspiration and motivation as well as guideposts toward how to begin. You'll also get a sense of the cold, hard realities associated with being your own boss.

This book is about the self-inventory you should take before you go into business for yourself to determine whether you have or could develop the fundamentals needed for success in any entrepreneurial endeavor. Do you have the passion, the work ethic, the people skills, and the courage?

Finally, you'll receive sage advice and guidance from a variety of people who are in various stages of building their own businesses. Each one of us is vastly different and in a different stage on our journey, but we have all learned a lot and want to share our knowledge and insights with you.

What will you *not* get out of this book? You won't learn how to be a better dancer if you want to become a dance teacher. You won't improve your writing if you want to become a writer. This book is not about how to sell things on the internet and become a millionaire, although that could become a part of your plan, rather it is about the essential qualities it takes to turn your passion and interests into an ability to freelance or build an enterprise. It's about learning how others have managed to create their own businesses, spanning the gamut from outdoor recreation to in-home service to brick-and-mortar businesses to freelance consulting from home.

The truth is we are experiencing a boom in entrepreneurship. Everyday, there are more examples of people who have started businesses out of a desire to make a difference or escape a bad work environment, and their passion and work habits have been key to their success.

I promise after reading this book, you will have the perspective and the insights required to make one of the most momentous decisions of your life: whether or not to go into business for yourself.

Don't be the worker who is hiding in his cubicle hoping to avoid the next round of layoffs. Don't be the employee who just assumes everything will be fine and nothing will ever change until the day she receives a pink slip. Don't be like I was before making the leap and remain stuck in a job that gives you only stress, heartache, and depression.

Instead, be smart by being prepared. Keep reading, and begin learning and planning for a future that could provide more security, and most certainly will provide more fulfillment than a job that feels like a daily grind.

Living an Independent Life requires, at times, gritting your teeth, holding back the tears, and quelling the urge to give a sarcastic comeback to a rude customer. It means never giving up. And guess what? You won't want to give up because you will love what you are doing 95 percent of the time! In fact, 97 percent of people making their primary living through self-employment say they do not plan to go back to a traditional job[7].

---

[7] Moulton, Cary, and Dave Cosgrave. "Second Annual Self-Employment Report." Freshbooks cloud accounting, February 21, 2018. https://www.freshbooks.com/_themes/freshbooks/brand-assets/2018selfemploymentreport.pdf.

Even when times are lean, you will find sustenance in the enjoyment of what you do for a living, on your own terms.

CHAPTER 1

WHAT IS AN INDEPENDENT LIFE?

"If you're happy in what you're doing, you'll like yourself, you'll have inner peace. And if you have that, along with physical health, you will have had more success than you could possibly have imagined."

-Johnny Carson, comedian and former host of *The Tonight Show*[8]

Deep down, we all recognize that we should earn money to live, not live to earn money. Yet how many of us end up feeling as if our work is meaningless and it's just to earn the dollars that can pay the bills

[8] Carson, Johnny. 2018. "Johnny Carson Quotes." BrainyQuote.Com. 2018. https://www.brainyquote.com/quotes/johnny_carson_393392.

and give us a bit of spending money on the week-ends?

I had that feeling times 10 in the early 2000s. After more than 15 years in natural resource conservation, I began a second career in teaching. I made the switch because I thought it would work best for me and my daughter, whom I was raising on my own.

If the school system had left me in the role of high school biology teacher, I would probably still be teaching to this day. I was passionate about what I did, engaging the kids. Unfortunately, despite the tremendous lip service paid to the uniqueness and individual learning styles of children in America's schools, that attitude does not extend to teachers. The reality is that most teachers are moved around among positions like interchangeable widgets, based primarily on seniority.

When my school's enrollment took a downturn, I lost my role as a biology teacher to a young woman who'd been hired one year ahead of me. She admitted to me that she did not care what she taught but would prefer driver's ed. I wound up teaching science and English to middle schoolers—a grade level I dreaded—in a struggling school.

I became depressed, went on antidepressants, and gained 20 pounds over the next three years. Some of the very best years of my daughter's life, from age 5 to 9 years old, were the worst years of mine, and I will never get that time back. Those years when I was stressed all the time, short-tempered, or so mindlessly focused on getting the next lesson plan done that I had very little time to spare—the memory of those years makes me sad to this day.

Finally, I quit out of sheer desperation because I truly felt that if I kept working in that particular school system, it would kill me. It felt like saving my own life.

Yet I was jumping off a cliff into thin air without a parachute. Not something I would ever recommend. I didn't have any jobs lined up. I didn't even have any interviews lined up.

I had a tiny bit of freelance work on the side, but I was not at all certain it could ever get to the point of supporting me. So my entry into the Independent Life was an act of desperation, and I hope you never get to that place in your own life.

The upside of the Independent Life

Making the switch to an Independent Life means you can reverse your situation and gain satisfaction in three major ways. First, by becoming your own boss. Second, through the full expression of your craft—whatever it is—and your creativity. Third, achieving your full potential to be a force for good in the world.

What do I mean by the Independent Life? The Independent Life is one where you are self-employed or run a small business, you make a good living, and you are free to be your own boss. The Independent Life also means that you have the responsibility of being a self-starter who:

- takes the initiative to make things happen
- sets your own goals
- finds clients
- comes up with ideas
- sets your own high standards for your work
- figures out how to solve problems and learns from your experience
- calculates risk and reward
- learns and improves continuously
- finds social support in ways alternative to the traditional workplace
- retools when things aren't working

Being your own boss means making the decisions and taking the risks that will help your business, your enterprise, your consultancy to grow. It means setting your own fees—and then finding the clients willing to pay them.

It's about having flexibility in your time schedule to plan your work hours around the needs of your clients, yes, but also around your own needs—whether that means time for your kids, time for doctor's appointments, or time (eventually) for that road trip you always wanted to take. It means, in some cases, the ability to work from home if that is what you prefer, or it could mean working from an office-share space, a coffee shop, or a truck!

In this book, I will share wisdom and lessons learned from 11 "Independent Lifers," including myself, who have made the leap and are in various stages of running their own businesses. These case studies, which you can download in full at kgreggelliott.com, include:

- Corey the Financial Services Professional
- Dan the Handyman
- Ivan the Cinematographer
- Maurrean the App Developer
- Melanie & José the Sport Fishing Entrepreneurs
- Misha the Ballroom Studio Owner
- Nigel the Nature Tour Leader
- Pam the Gym Owner
- Sophie the Wildlife Artist
- Gregg the Conservation Communications Consultant (and author of this book)

We have all been there, at the very beginning, plagued by doubts, not knowing if our ventures would be successful. Everyone I interviewed expressed great generosity and a willingness to share what they have learned as a way of reaching out a helping hand to the "next person in line." I am deeply grateful for their time and friendship.

Expressing your own superpower

The Independent Life means that you will finally be able to fully express yourself through your work. It is, after all, your business: everything about it will reflect some aspect of yourself, from your website to your highlighted skills and talents to your end product and the type of clients you attract.

When you are running your own business, you will experience the satisfaction of a job well done in a way that does not happen when you are working for someone else. Even if you are part of a team or your product is one small part of a much larger whole, you get to produce and fully express your creativity, skill, and craftsmanship through your part.

This does *not* mean that you won't collaborate and make adjustments based on the input of others—that is almost always the path to success. It does mean that your business is wholly you and reflects your standards, values, and workmanship.

Even when subcontracting out some of your work or hiring employees, the way that those people express themselves in their work is guided by you. Your enterprise will finally allow—no, require—that you attend to every aspect of what you produce. You will meet a new and fascinating variety of people through your chosen profession, and you will have at least one very important thing in common with everyone that you meet through work: a clear interest in your chosen field.

When you run your own business, you are constantly learning because the world is constantly changing, and to survive you have to adjust. You'll be problem solving and learning how to accomplish tasks you might never have considered before, such as marketing or accounting or bank negotiations or the proliferating number of tools online available to run a business.

Above all, working for yourself at a profession that you have chosen is one of the best ways for you to express your fullest potential in life. You get to choose your "superpower."

When you work for yourself in a craft or industry or cause that you are passionate about, it unleashes your true potential to be a force for good in the world. That is the best that any of us can really ask for in life, isn't it?

For me, this has been the most powerful aspect of my sole proprietorship. I'm a communications consultant, which means I do everything from strategic planning to writing to e-news and social media—all focused on conservation of wildlife and their habitats. My clients are mostly government agencies and non-profits. My business was an outgrowth of years of experience in a variety of nonprofit jobs, including a stint as a Nature Conservancy preserve manager in California.

Because I believe so passionately in the importance of the natural world and our duty to be good stewards of the planet, my work gives me satisfaction every day, no matter whether I am writing a strategic plan or a short paragraph about forestry research. As my website says, "No task is too small when the purpose is large."

Misha, another Independent Lifer, runs a ballroom dance studio. To some, that may sound like a trivial way in which to be a force for good in the world. Peace through paso doblé? In reality, nothing could be further from the truth. Dance is such an all-consuming passion for the people who enjoy it, that they call his studio their "happy place." What could be more meaningful in life than giving others unadulterated joy?

Dan the Handyman, another Independent Lifer, uses the tagline "Quality service at a reasonable price." He uses his considerable skills to allow people living in middle class and working class neighborhoods to maintain what is probably their most precious investment, their home. He's increasing the quality of his community one new tile floor at a time.

An Independent Life is also one in which 100 percent of the time invested in your enterprise will come back to benefit you, and indirectly, your clients and customers. In many cases, when you put in more hours, you'll actually make more money, something that cannot be said for many jobs. I have learned that earning potential is a powerful motivator!

Let's talk business

If the word "business" makes you shudder, if you have never thought of yourself as a "business person," if you are saying to yourself, "I have no knowledge of business and no training," well then join the club! None of the people I listed at the beginning of this chapter went to business school either.

I never had any interest in business because to my younger self, it reeked of profit-chasing and greed and selling boring widgets just to make money. Economics taught me that pollution was an "externality" that did not have to be taken into account when calculating wealth, an idea I derided. An accounting spreadsheet seemed like Greek to me (and still does to be honest).

There is a difference between "business" the way most university programs define it and "entrepreneurship." When we hear the word business, we often think of large corporations, Wall Street, or the short-term drive to maximize profits. A business degree is designed fundamentally to teach people how to manage organizations.

An entrepreneur, on the other hand, is "an individual who starts and runs a business with limited resources and planning, and is responsible for all the risks and rewards of his or her business venture."[9]

When you take your skill set, your body of knowledge, or your idea and put it to work to help achieve something you are passionate about, it's nothing like fitting into the culture of a large organization where so many jobs are concentrated.

As Maurrean the App Developer says, "When you go to work for other companies, you have to put a part of your spirit to sleep while at work to fit the corporate structure and values. You have to play the corporate political game so that you will not be disliked at work and can (maybe) keep your job. When you work for yourself, it gives you an opportunity to explore, discover, and nurture who you were meant to be."

There is nothing wrong with making a profit, indeed it's essential. Work, at its core, is about making a

---

[9] Seth, Shobhit. "Entrepreneurs and Entrepreneurship Defined." Investopedia, September 25, 2014.
https://www.investopedia.com/articles/investing/092514/entrepreneur-vs-small-business-owner-defined.asp.

trade that benefits both sides in the exchange by supporting survival or quality of life. It's taking what you have (skills, ideas, hard work) and trading it for what someone else has (usually in the form of money, which they have received for their own skills, ideas, hard work). If you cannot make ends meet through your work, then not much else matters. All the passion in the world is not going to put food on your table or gas in your tank.

However, work is far *more* than only making a profit, something that many large corporations seem to have forgotten. The wonderful thing about the Independent Life is that it allows you to focus on what is important or of interest to you while also providing a livelihood.

Waking up

Building an Independent Life also means that you bear 100 percent of the responsibility for your success or failure. It means you will reap the rewards when a decision pays off but also suffer the consequences when a calculated risk leads to a loss. It means you'll often be learning things "the hard way," as I tell my daughter, by making your own mistakes. This can be scary. It can also be exhilarating!

Running your own ship makes you realize that although you are responsible for what you do, you are not in control. You can only control your actions and the quality of your work, but you can't control the ocean of other factors out there in the business environment.

This realization wakes you up because you understand in a visceral way that you are skating on the fine edge between circumstance and opportunity. You understand you are never fully in control, and the world will toss both hand grenades and diamonds in your path.

But this understanding has the paradoxical effect of making you readier than you have ever been to take necessary risks. You understand that this is the true nature of life: taking what comes and making the best of it by being your very best to the limits of your ability. There are no guarantees.

Living an Independent Life means you will have truly lived by striving to achieve your full potential as an individual.

Moving from a place of desperation to an Independent Life

Somehow, after I quit my job as a teacher, I was able to move from that place of despair to a place of independence and confidence over the next nine years. I have arrived at what I believe is a much more balanced way of living.

Although I'm intelligent, committed, and passionate about what I do, I'm nothing extraordinary. I haven't made a million dollars or invented anything. I'm not the latest, greatest company that you read about in the tech section of the newspaper. I am probably a lot like you, and my feeling is if I can do it, so can you—as long as you possess or are willing to develop a few key qualities.

So how did I make it? Immediately after quitting, I called up the man that I had been freelancing for on the side, who also happened to be someone that I had worked for previously in my natural resource conservation career. I told him what I had done, and he offered me a job on the spot.

However, the job he offered was contract work, and truthfully it did not pay that much. After adding in self-employment taxes, my own health care insurance, plus the cost of covering my own vacation and sick time (there would be no dollars left for retirement), I would make somewhat less than I had been earning as a teacher (which I probably do not have to tell you was not much).

But it was a chance to go back to my passion, environmental conservation, and it was a chance for an Independent Life—something I did not truly appreciate at the time. Here I am ten years later, still in business, 20 pounds lighter, frequently enthralled and challenged, much much happier, and making far more than I ever could have as a teacher.

This book is not about how to make a million dollars and retire by the age of 40, although I'm certain some of you may do that. In fact, roughly half of those who are successfully self-employed plan to work through their retirement years by choice! I'm older than 40 as I write this, and I'm as happy as I have ever been in my life because I do work that matters to me a great deal. I am my own boss, and I make enough income to support myself, my daughter, and a flexible lifestyle that includes some great travel each year. That's the Independent Life.

The real-life lessons catalogued in this book were hard-won. Successful entrepreneurs have a good work ethic, and because we have passion we always try to do the best for our clients and customers. However, the reality is there's a lot to learn and we all make mistakes.

This book is designed to help you in four ways:

- It will give you an overview of three mega-trends that are already changing the work landscape in the U.S. and around the world.
- It will present four core elements, or criteria, that all of the 10 Independent Lifers I interviewed agree are essential for someone who

wants to successfully create and grow their own enterprise.

- It will provide some key principles for success by showing how others have succeeded, while also helping you to avoid some of the beginner mistakes that we all make.
- It will give you an overview of job and business opportunities in the near future that are foreseen by workplace experts.

We will begin at the beginning: the problem with jobs.

PART I

THE COMING JOBAGEDDON: THE WHY OF SELF-EMPLOYMENT

CHAPTER 2

AMERICA'S CORPORATE JOB COMPACT IS OVER

"If you live for the weekends and vacations, your shit is broken."

-Gary Vaynerchuk, entrepreneur, speaker, and CEO of VaynerMedia[10]

Dan had been in his new position as Quality Manager at an appliance manufacturing plant in Memphis, Tennessee when he took a vacation to Orange Beach on the Gulf Coast in early June of 2016. He returned, sun-tanned and relaxed, on a Friday and went into the office on his last day off just so he

---

[10] Hughes, Chris. 2016. "10 Inspirational Gary Vaynerchuk Quotes." Chris Hughes (blog). September 2, 2016.
https://medium.com/@whosChrisHughes/10-inspirational-gary-vaynerchuk-quotes-6ac9113e7c11.

would not start the week behind on the following Monday. That Friday, HR called Dan to tell him his position had been cut and he was out of a job, victim of the latest Reduction in Force.

Sara had worked for years in the hospitality industry, employed as an accountant for one of the largest hotel chains in America. She was moving up and had recently accepted a position where she would scope out potential sites for new hotel franchises. Then the hotel chain was purchased and taken over by a completely new company. Sara's job was cut in the downsizing that followed.

Most of us have heard at least one, if not many, stories like Dan's or Sara's. Their stories symbolize everything that's wrong with corporate America and have become all-too-common scenarios for millions of Americans over the past generation. According to one study at the John J. Heldrich Center for Workforce Development at Rutgers University, from 2009 to 2014 alone, fully one-fifth of American workers were laid off[11].

Perhaps this is your story, or perhaps you wonder if this could happen to you.

---

[11] Puzzanghera, Jim. "One-Fifth of U.S. Workers Were Laid off in Past Five Years, Study Says." *Los Angeles Times*. September 24, 2014, sec. Business. http://www.latimes.com/business/la-fi-layoffs-unemployment-jobs-economy-20140924-story.html.

Hard work, dedication, and years of experience do not go very far to ensure job security anymore. In fact, 63 percent of workers now believe they will have a more secure future working for themselves than relying on the corporate job market[12].

The story does not end there, however.

Unbeknownst to Sara, another woman—we'll call her Amelia—in the same city had also worked for the same hotel chain for decades, moving up into a position of authority within the IT side of the reservations branch. Amelia survived the downsizing, but her assessment of the situation was scathing.

"The new company gets rid of all these people so they can cut costs and bring in their own people who don't know anything about our company. Then because we actually needed our people to get work done, it creates problems that have to be solved."

Amelia's observation summarizes the drastic changes that have made the necessity to find new employment a more and more common task in America.

[12] Upwork, Freelancers Union. "Freelancing in America: 2017 Survey - Upwork." Upwork, October 27, 2017.
https://www.upwork.com/i/freelancing-in-america/2017/.

The evolving meaning of "job" in America

Much of the story of how the corporate "contract" with American workers has disintegrated over the past 60 to 70 years is vividly captured in Rick Wartzman's book, *The End of Loyalty*[13]. Understanding the history of work in America provides an eye-opening context for how much the value of a job to so many workers in America has declined. Without this context, you might not even realize how different jobs are today compared to your parents' and grandparents' generations.

According to Warzman, a "Golden Age" age of employment in the U.S. began at the end of the Second World War, marked by an understanding between labor and corporate leaders that greater employment led to greater prosperity for the country. This mid-20th century model of a capitalism that took care of its workers included pensions, health insurance, and an effort to provide job security in return for lifelong loyalty to the company. However, within half a century, that understanding would be turned on its head.

Beginning in the 1970s, deindustrialization—the transition of the American economy from manufacturing to knowledge-based jobs—boosted unemployment rates to a post-war high of 11 percent in 1982. Automation and the digital revolution's knowledge-based

---

[13] Wartzman, Rick. *The End of Loyalty, the Rise and Fall of Good Jobs in America.* New York: Public Affairs, 2017.

economy, plus offshoring of jobs to decrease labor costs, were largely responsible for the job loss.

However, also beginning in the 1970s, a new corporate model rose to popularity, marked by the philosophy that a corporation's greatest social responsibility was to increase profits for shareholders (but in the context of open and free competition and without fraud).[14] This led to the kind of business practices that eliminated Dan's and Sara's job and made Amelia roll her eyes.

Business leaders increasingly saw employment as an avoidable expense, a sharp departure from the view that greater employment equals greater prosperity. Creating "shareholder value" is often at odds with maintaining stable employment because employee cutbacks look good in quarterly reports and can often boost stock prices, at least temporarily.[15]

Job cutbacks continued, and by 1990 the number of people employed by Fortune 500 companies had dropped to fewer than 12.5 million from nearly 16 million a decade before. The desire to maximize shareholder profits (measured via stock prices for publicly held companies) led to further cost-cutting measures.

---

[14] Wartzman, Rick. *The End of Loyalty, the Rise and Fall of Good Jobs in America*. New York: Public Affairs, 2017.
[15] Abraham, Stephan. "Layoffs And The Stock Market." Investopedia, January 2, 2013. https://www.investopedia.com/stock-analysis/2013/layoffs-and-the-stock-market-c-hpq0123.aspx.

These measures included development of 401k employee retirement funds. Although 401k's were more portable than pensions, facilitating movement between jobs, they also put the burden and the risk of saving sufficiently for retirement onto employees, clearing many of those liabilities from the corporate books.

Likewise, whereas paid health insurance was once part of the standard job package in the U.S., companies began shoveling these costs onto employees through co-pays and higher deductibles.[16]

Take this job and shove it

In the 1950s, America's Golden Age for work, wages and salaries climbed for almost everyone, up 54 percent overall for full-time blue- and white-collar workers, and outpacing inflation. That trend ended in 1974, when a 2 percent dip in American wages marked the beginning of a four-decade period in which people's paychecks would barely get any bigger once inflation was taken into account.[17]

This decline in wages over the past four decades has taken place even as worker productivity (meaning, ultimately, the amount of profits they are able to gen-

[16] Wartzman, Rick. *The End of Loyalty, the Rise and Fall of Good Jobs in America*. New York: Public Affairs, 2017.
[17] Wartzman, Rick. *The End of Loyalty, the Rise and Fall of Good Jobs in America*. New York: Public Affairs, 2017.

erate) has increased. Specifically, from 1973 to 2013, hourly compensation of a typical non-supervisory worker rose just 9 percent while productivity increased 74 percent![18]

Workers produced much more, but typical workers' pay lagged far behind
Disconnect between productivity and typical worker's compensation, 1948–2013

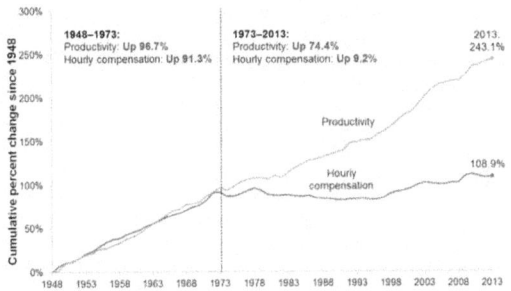

Note: Data are for compensation (wages and benefits) of production/nonsupervisory workers in the private sector and net productivity of the total economy. "Net productivity" is the growth of output of goods and services less depreciation per hour worked.

Source: EPI analysis of Bureau of Labor Statistics and Bureau of Economic Analysis data

Updated from Figure A in *Raising America's Pay: Why It's Our Central Economic Policy Challenge*

Economic Policy Institute

Reprinted with permission from the Economic Policy Institute, *Wage Stagnation in Nine Charts*, January 6, 2015.

---

[18] Mishel, Lawrence, Elise Gould, and Josh Bivens. "Wage Stagnation in Nine Charts." *Economic Policy Institute* (blog), January 6, 2015. https://www.epi.org/publication/charting-wage-stagnation/.

Are you willing to work at will?

Jobs in America are now mere ghosts of their former selves. Many are "at will," meaning employees can be dismissed without cause and without notice, as long as the reason behind the dismissal is not illegal (for example, racial or sex discrimination).

Many jobs require several years of work before the employer will contribute any match to an employee's retirement 401k, and just turn on the radio to hear about the latest increases in health care insurance premiums coming your way. Is it any wonder that the majority of independent workers believe that having diversified sources of income is more secure than relying on one job?[19]

It turns out, jobageddon is a slow-moving juggernaut that has been sneaking up on us for quite a while. It started in the 1970s, picked up steam in the 1980s, and according to many experts, is headed toward warp speed.

Summary

America's Golden Age of employment—that period when company loyalty was repaid in the form of se-curity and benefits such as pensions and health in-

---

[19] Upwork, Freelancers Union. "Freelancing in America: 2017 Survey - Upwork." Upwork, October 27, 2017.
https://www.upwork.com/i/freelancing-in-america/2017/.

surance—is long over. Since the 1970s, increasing job insecurity, flat wages (when adjusted for inflation), and rising costs of health insurance have caused many people to seek new ways of making money. The "side hustle," or extra work in addition to the "day job," is suddenly popular, as is self-employment.

These days, if you want to receive the fruits of your own efforts, you are less and less likely to do so via a "middle class" job, the very thing that has been a defining part of the American dream since our country's founding.

All these changes pale in comparison to what is on the horizon: the Fourth Industrial Revolution. In Chapter 3, we will learn how business analysts are now fretting that new technologies could create a period of job loss and turmoil that may be unprecedented in the history of the world.

CHAPTER 3

ARTIFICIAL INTELLIGENCE: CENTAUR VS. MATRIX

"With artificial intelligence we are summoning the demon."

—Elon Musk, founder of SpaceX,
co-founder of Tesla[20]

Jobageddon won't take the form of a Terminator style droid. It will look more like a tiny clip or "shoe" that zips along a conveyor belt[21], or possibly a good ole

[20] Szoldra, Paul. "Elon Musk Thinks Sci-Fi Nightmare Scenarios About Artificial Intelligence Could Really Happen." *Business Insider*, October 24, 2014. http://www.businessinsider.com/elon-musk-artificial-intelligence-mit-2014-10.

[21] Kitroeff, Natalie. "Where Internet Orders Mean Real Jobs, and New Life for Communities." *The New York Times*, October 22, 2017, sec. Economy. https://www.nytimes.com/2017/10/22/business/economy/warehouse-jobs.html.

computer. Only this computer won't just do spread-
sheets, word processing, and the internet at your di-
rection—it will write your story for you if you're a
journalist[22].

Jobageddon could take the form of self-driving trucks
that eliminate the need for drivers[23], a four-armed robot that disrupts the way in which doctors learn surgery[24], or drones[25] and "roomba" type machines[26] that
change the way farmers control weeds.

In case you haven't already heard, we are at the
dawn of the Fourth Industrial Revolution, the age of
digitalization, robotics, and artificial intelligence[27].
Let's unpack those terms.

[22] Graefe, Andreas. "How Algorithms and Human Journalists Will Need to
Work Together." The Conversation. Accessed March 18, 2018.
http://theconversation.com/how-algorithms-and-human-journalists-will-
need-to-work-together-81869.

[23] Balakrishnana, Anita. 2017. "Goldman Sachs Analysis of Autonomous
Vehicle Job Loss." CNBC.com. May 22, 2017.
https://www.cnbc.com/2017/05/22/goldman-sachs-analysis-of-autonomous-
vehicle-job-loss.html.

[24] Beane, Matt. "Young Doctors Struggle to Learn Robotic Surgery – so
They Are Practicing in the Shadows." The Conversation. Accessed March
26, 2018. http://theconversation.com/young-doctors-struggle-to-learn-
robotic-surgery-so-they-are-practicing-in-the-shadows-89646.

[25] Mazur, Michal. 2016. "Six Ways Drones Are Revolutionizing Agriculture."
MIT Technology Review, July 20, 2016.
https://www.technologyreview.com/s/601935/six-ways-drones-are-
revolutionizing-agriculture/.

[26] Dawson, Gloria. 2013. "Lettuce Bot: Roomba for Weeds." Modern-
farmer.com. Modern Farmer (blog). May 16, 2013.
https://modernfarmer.com/2013/05/lettuce-bot-roomba-for-weeds/.

[27] World Economic Forum. "The Future of Jobs." World Economic Forum,
January 2016. http://www3.weforum.org/docs/WEF_Future_of_Jobs.pdf.

Digitalization (in contrast to digitization) is the process of employing digital technologies and information to improve or transform business operations. Examples are when workplaces move from file cabinets to computerized databases or how an architect who used to produce hand-drawn schematics now uses computer-aided design (CAD) to design digitally. Digitization, on the other hand, is simply what happens when we take analog data and turn it into 1s and 0s. Digitization is a necessary prerequisite of digitalization.[28]

Robots are machines that can accomplish a complex set of tasks automatically, usually through computerized programming. Robotics is a rapidly advancing field that has already been used extensively to automate manufacturing, and is advancing into the realms of science fiction with the aid of artificial Intelligence, or AI.

Artificial Intelligence, or AI, is a collection of advanced technologies that allows machines to sense, comprehend, act, and learn. AI includes machine learning, which provides systems with the ability to learn and improve at tasks without being explicitly programmed.[29]

---

[28] Clerck, J.-P. De. "Digitization, Digitalization and Digital Transformation: The Differences." i-SCOOP, July 25, 2016. https://www.i-scoop.eu/digitization-digitalization-digital-transformation-disruption/.

[29] Accenture. "Artificial Intelligence | Accenture." Accessed March 26, 2018. https://www.accenture.com/us-en/artificial-intelligence-index.

One-third of work hours in America could be automated

AI combined with the field of robotics is advancing automation as well as creating "cognitive" robots that mimic human behavior. Job automation allows machines to complete tasks more efficiently, effectively, and above all, more cheaply than you or I could.

In a major assessment of automation issued in 2017 by business research giant McKinsey Global Institute entitled *Jobs Lost, Jobs Gained*,[30] the experts predict that up to one-third of work activities across 46 countries could be replaced by automation by the year 2030. Automation will change even more occupations than it will displace: right now up to six in 10 jobs are made up of activities of which about 30 percent could be automated.

Perhaps you are thinking that in advanced countries, like the U.S., where service and information jobs are more common, you don't have to worry about your own personal jobpocalypse. Think again. Advanced economies will have a higher incentive to automate because we have higher wage rates. As many as

---

[30] Manyika, James, Susan Lund, Michael Chui, Jacques Bughin, Jonathan Woetzel, Parul Batra, Ryan Ko, and Saurabh Sanghvi. "Jobs Lost, Jobs Gained," December 2017. https://www.mckinsey.com/global-themes/future-of-organizations-and-work/what-the-future-of-work-will-mean-for-jobs-skills-and-wages.

one-quarter of work hours in the U.S. could be automated by the year 2030.[31]

Does 2030 seem too far into the future for you? A 2016 report from the World Economic Forum, based on a survey of Human Resource chiefs representing more than 13 million employees across nine broad industry sectors in 15 countries around the world found that respondents expect these trends to impact jobs within the next five years.[32] That brings jobagaddon to about year 2021!

A global survey in 2017 of more than 5,400 business and IT executives across 31 countries found that 85 percent of executives will invest extensively in AI-related technologies over the next three years.[33]

Centaur vs. Matrix

Will AI lead us into a dystopian, Matrix-like future where we become slaves to robots? Or will it lead us to a utopia where advanced human/machine hybrids

---

[31] Manyika, James, Susan Lund, Michael Chui, Jacques Bughin, Jonathan Woetzel, Parul Batra, Ryan Ko, and Saurabh Sanghvi. "Jobs Lost, Jobs Gained," December 2017. https://www.mckinsey.com/global-themes/future-of-organizations-and-work/what-the-future-of-work-will-mean-for-jobs-skills-and-wages.
[32] World Economic Forum. "The Future of Jobs." World Economic Forum, January 2016. http://www3.weforum.org/docs/WEF_Future_of_Jobs.pdf.
[33] Accenture. "Technology Vision 2017." Accenture LLP. Accessed March 18, 2018. https://www.accenture.com/t20170321T032507__w__/us-en/_acnmedia/Accenture/next-gen-4/tech-vision-2017/pdf/Accenture-TV17-Full.pdf.

known as "centaurs" are better, go farther, and think smarter than either one working alone?

The centaur vision of the future builds on the little known result that occurred in the year after an AI computer first beat Gary Kasparov at chess. In 1998, a human-AI team was able to defeat, not only a strictly human team but a solo AI as well. The centaur future focuses on AI's "forgotten cousin," IA, or Intelligence Augmentation, a science that actively seeks to forge AI tools for the purpose of expanding and enlarging human intellectual capabilities.[34]

An equally hopeful view of the future envisions that, in the long-term, AI "will not only contribute to dynamic economies that create jobs, but also help create the economic surpluses that will enable societies to address . . . workforce transitions."[35]

Elon Musk, founder of SpaceX (working to take commercial space flights to Mars) and creator of the Tesla (an electric car with the hardware for self-driving already built-in) has great exposure to cutting-edge AI, and he is concerned.

---

[34] Case, Nicky. "How To Become A Centaur." *Journal of Design and Science*, February 6, 2018. https://jods.mitpress.mit.edu/pub/issue3-case.

[35] Manyika, James, Susan Lund, Michael Chui, Jacques Bughin, Jonathan Woetzel, Parul Batra, Ryan Ko, and Saurabh Sanghvi. "Jobs Lost, Jobs Gained," December 2017. https://www.mckinsey.com/global-themes/future-of-organizations-and-work/what-the-future-of-work-will-mean-for-jobs-skills-and-wages.

He has neatly summed up the matrix aspect of a future with AI: "There certainly will be job disruption. Because what's going to happen is robots will be able to do everything better than us . . . I mean all of us. Yeah, I am not sure exactly what to do about this. This is really the scariest problem to me, I will tell you."[36]

He is concerned enough that he founded OpenAI, a non-profit artificial intelligence research company with a mission to "ensure that artificial general intelligence (AGI)—by which we mean highly autonomous systems that outperform humans at most economically valuable work—benefits all of humanity."[37]

So what does all this turmoil translate into for those of us already in the work force and those just entering it? McKinsey Global Institute predicts that by 2030, anywhere from 75 million to 375 million workers (3 to 15 percent of the global workforce) will have to switch the type of job they do, with the highest share of these in advanced economies. Almost all of us will need to adapt.[38]

---

[36] Clifford, Catherine. "9 Mind-Blowing Things Elon Musk Said about Robots and AI in 2017," December 18, 2017. https://www.cnbc.com/2017/12/18/9-mind-blowing-things-elon-musk-said-about-robots-and-ai-in-2017.html.

[37] OpenAI. "OpenAI Charter." OpenAI Blog, April 9, 2018. https://blog.openai.com/openai-charter/.

[38] Manyika, James, Susan Lund, Michael Chui, Jacques Bughin, Jonathan Woetzel, Parul Batra, Ryan Ko, and Saurabh Sanghvi. "Jobs Lost, Jobs Gained," December 2017. https://www.mckinsey.com/global-themes/future-of-organizations-and-work/what-the-future-of-work-will-mean-for-jobs-skills-and-wages.

Will this time be different?

The Fourth Industrial Revolution will differ from earlier transitions because it will not involve young people deserting the countryside, moving to the big city and the big time. Rather, it will involve huge changes in the existing workforce.

The challenge for employers will be to retrain their workers, but guess what? The level of job retraining that will be required has never been encountered, or accomplished, in the history of the world. Up to one-third of the U.S. workforce may need to be retrained![39]

While researching this topic, I knew I was really on to something when I read the portion of the McKinsey Global Institute report that cited Friedrich Engels to explain anticipated trends in the workplace. Engels, you may recall, worked alongside Karl Marx to create Marxism![40]

The report cited the "Engels pause"—a nearly 50-year period during the 19th century Industrial Revolution when, largely due to new technologies, worker

---

[39] Manyika, James, Susan Lund, Michael Chui, Jacques Bughin, Jonathan Woetzel, Parul Batra, Ryan Ko, and Saurabh Sanghvi. "Jobs Lost, Jobs Gained," December 2017. https://www.mckinsey.com/global-themes/future-of-organizations-and-work/what-the-future-of-work-will-mean-for-jobs-skills-and-wages.

[40] Marx, Karl, and Friedrich Engels. 1848. The Communist Manifesto. 12th Media Services. https://www.amazon.com/Communist-Manifesto-Karl-Marx/dp/1680922106/ref=tmm_hrd_swatch_0?_encoding=UTF8&qid=&sr=.

productivity (and profits) grew rapidly while workers' wages stayed flat.[41] That "pause" helped to spawn a revolution in Russia.

Now there is a debate, ongoing among the scholars who study work, about whether this time our Fourth Industrial revolution will be "different"—and not in a good way. That's because the current wave of new technologies will allow machines to perform some work that requires *thinking*, including the ability to learn and improve at particular tasks without much human assistance.

McKinsey Global Institute reports that automation, robotics, and AI could veer from the paths of earlier waves of technology disruption in two ways:

(1) the speed of technological development and progress in machine learning and

(2) the potential to displace a large share of the work force in a relatively short time if the adoption of automation is rapid.[42]

---

[41] Manyika, James, Susan Lund, Michael Chui, Jacques Bughin, Jonathan Woetzel, Parul Batra, Ryan Ko, and Saurabh Sanghvi. "Jobs Lost, Jobs Gained," December 2017. https://www.mckinsey.com/global-themes/future-of-organizations-and-work/what-the-future-of-work-will-mean-for-jobs-skills-and-wages.

[42] Manyika, James, Susan Lund, Michael Chui, Jacques Bughin, Jonathan Woetzel, Parul Batra, Ryan Ko, and Saurabh Sanghvi. "Jobs Lost, Jobs Gained," December 2017. https://www.mckinsey.com/global-themes/future-of-organizations-and-work/what-the-future-of-work-will-mean-for-jobs-skills-and-wages.

Every wave of automation is likely to affect more complex tasks, so both high wage and low wage workers will be affected. According to one MIT expert on the digital economy, executives are underestimating the speed, scope, and scale of the disruption that AI will bring.[43]

The late Stephen Hawking, a brilliant physicist best known for his work on black holes and the theory of relativity, put it this way: "The automation of factories has already decimated jobs in traditional manufacturing, and the rise of artificial intelligence is likely to extend this job destruction deep into the middle classes, with only the most caring, creative, or supervisory roles remaining."[44]

The "hollowing" of the American workplace

If this all sounds a bit too "Matrix" for you, then think about what has already happened in the American workplace. In Chapter 1 we reviewed the decline of the corporate job compact in America and the corresponding decline of the middle class. One of the pri-

---

[43] Kirkland, Rik. "Competing in the AI Economy: An Interview with MIT's Andrew McAfee | McKinsey & Company." McKinsey & Company, March 2018. https://www.mckinsey.com/business-functions/mckinsey-analytics/our-insights/competing-in-the-ai-economy-an-interview-with-mits-andrew-mcafee.

[44] Hawking, Stephen. "This Is the Most Dangerous Time for Our Planet | Stephen Hawking | Opinion | The Guardian." *The Guardian*, December 1, 2016. https://www.theguardian.com/commentisfree/2016/dec/01/stephen-hawking-dangerous-time-planet-inequality.

mary contributors to this decline has been digitalization.

In 2017 the Brookings Institution analyzed 545 occupations covering 90 percent of the U.S. workforce in all industries since 2001. Their analysis shows that from 2002 to 2016 the shares of U.S. jobs and employment that require substantial digital knowledge rose rapidly, particularly in the fields of financial management, human resources, the legal profession, automotive industry, nursing, die and tool makers, welders, and other construction jobs.[45]

Since the 1980s, digitalization has created essentially a "hollowing" effect in the job market, increasing jobs at the high and low skill levels, but hollowing out the middle. What we have now in the U.S. is a two-tiered labor market. Between 2005 and 2014, fully two-thirds of income groups in the U.S. had either flat or falling income (from wages and investments).[46]

With manufacturing jobs increasingly either automated or offshored, people with fewer skills have been shifting to service jobs such as tending corporate flower beds, working at Wendy's, taking care of the

[45] Muro, Mark, Sifan Liu, Jacob Whiton, and Siddharth Kulkarni. "Digitalization and the American Workforce." The Brookings Institution, November 2017. https://www.brookings.edu/research/digitalization-and-the-american-workforce/.

[46] Manyika, James, Susan Lund, Michael Chui, Jacques Bughin, Jonathan Woetzel, Parul Batra, Ryan Ko, and Saurabh Sanghvi. "Jobs Lost, Jobs Gained," December 2017. https://www.mckinsey.com/global-themes/future-of-organizations-and-work/what-the-future-of-work-will-mean-for-jobs-skills-and-wages.

ill, or guarding property—which all tend to be lower paying. "Idea-intensive" jobs—those that create new products, advance healthcare, research new drugs, or whip up the latest Hollywood concoction—have been gaining a larger share of corporate profits and income.[47]

As we saw in Chapter 2, productivity and incomes have become disconnected. Americans have experienced flat wages over the past four decades even as worker productivity (along with the amount of profits they are able to generate) has increased. This trend could be exacerbated by increases in productivity associated with AI and automation.

Embracing both technology and education

Don't get me wrong. I love my computer. Without my computer and the internet, I would not have the capacity to work as an Independent Lifer communications consultant.

So far, I've been on the winning side of digitalization, and my case illustrates several broader points. In the future, those most likely to achieve either Independent Lifer status or get "good jobs" will have college or associate's degrees.

---

[47] Manyika, James, Susan Lund, Michael Chui, Jacques Bughin, Jonathan Woetzel, Parul Batra, Ryan Ko, and Saurabh Sanghvi. "Jobs Lost, Jobs Gained," December 2017. https://www.mckinsey.com/global-themes/future-of-organizations-and-work/what-the-future-of-work-will-mean-for-jobs-skills-and-wages.

Since 1991, the share of "good jobs" (median income $55,000) going to workers without a bachelor's degree fell from 60 to 45 percent. "Good jobs in factories at the height of the manufacturing economy in the U.S. only required a high school education or less, but the new good jobs almost all require at least some postsecondary education and training. In fact, the number of workers in good jobs with only a high school diploma has declined by one million since 1991."[48]

Although success stories by people who have never finished college are increasingly in the news, McKinsey Global Institute calculated that in more than 800 occupations from 2016 to 2030, labor demand for those with a high school diploma will decrease from 1 to 7 percent. Those with an associate's degree will have a slight edge in advanced economies, with four-year and advanced college degrees seeing the greatest increase in demand, from 1 to 3 percent.[49]

Furthermore, the people who get good jobs will also be those who tend to embrace technology as well, as digitalization is a "key pathway to increased earn-

---

[48] Carnevale, Anthony, Jeff Strohl, Ban Cheah, and Neil Ridley. "Good Jobs Data." Georgetown University Center on Education and the Workforce, 2017. https://goodjobsdata.org/wp-content/uploads/Good-Jobs-wo-BA-final.pdf.
[49] Manyika, James, Susan Lund, Michael Chui, Jacques Bughin, Jonathan Woetzel, Parul Batra, Ryan Ko, and Saurabh Sanghvi. "Jobs Lost, Jobs Gained," December 2017. https://www.mckinsey.com/global-themes/future-of-organizations-and-work/what-the-future-of-work-will-mean-for-jobs-skills-and-wages.

ings,"[50] and 71 percent of freelancers agree that tech is enabling them to find or execute their work.[51]

What does this mean? It means that as the world gets more complicated and new technologies proliferate, education does matter, and I would argue that this applies to both self-employment and jobs. However, a college education is expensive, and one of the single most important ways of preparing to build your own business is to save money while avoiding debt. That's why more and more people are searching for alternatives to gain skills for the workplace.[52] A good resource for thinking along these lines is the book co-written by brothers Seth and Chandler Bolt, *Breaking out of a Broken System.*[53]

Is the news all bad?

No! The news is definitely not all bad. Yes, there will be potentially unprecedented turmoil in job markets in the coming decades, with some job functions eliminated entirely and others changing radically. How-

[50] Muro, Mark, and Sifan Liu On 11/27/17 at 11:31 AM. 2017. "The US Is Digitalizing at Warp Speed. What Could Possibly Go Wrong?" Newsweek, November 27, 2017. http://www.newsweek.com/us-digitalizing-warp-speed-what-could-possibly-go-wrong-723240.

[51] Upwork, Freelancers Union. "Freelancing in America: 2017 Survey - Upwork." Upwork, October 27, 2017. https://www.upwork.com/i/freelancing-in-america/2017/.

[52] Stephens, Dale J. "Do You Really Have to Go to College?" New York Times. *The Choice Blog* (blog), March 7, 2013. https://thechoice.blogs.nytimes.com/2013/03/07/do-you-really-have-to-go-to-college/.

[53] Bolt, Seth, and Chandler Bolt. 2014. Breaking Out Of A Broken System.

ever, new job creation could more than make up for jobs lost as a result of automation and AI, with 8 to 9 percent of jobs in 2030 likely to be in occupations that have yet to be created.[54]

The opportunities to keep working may very well depend on your ability to be flexible, embrace change, and learn new skills.

Here are some questions that are critical for you to consider:

- Will your current employer provide the retraining necessary for you to keep your job?
- Will your transformed job be one that you even want to keep?
- If you are in a job you already dislike, and change is coming anyway, isn't now a good time to take your destiny into your own hands?

It is the thesis of this book that one of the best ways to weather the changes that lie ahead is for those dissatisfied with their place in the job force to plan for or make a switch to working independently. With great change comes great opportunity.

---

[54] Manyika, James, Susan Lund, Michael Chui, Jacques Bughin, Jonathan Woetzel, Parul Batra, Ryan Ko, and Saurabh Sanghvi. "Jobs Lost, Jobs Gained," December 2017. https://www.mckinsey.com/global-themes/future-of-organizations-and-work/what-the-future-of-work-will-mean-for-jobs-skills-and-wages.

Summary

We've seen how experts around the world focusing on work issues agree that Artificial Intelligence, or AI, combined with robotics, and more generally the broad digitalization of the workplace are combining to create the world's Fourth Industrial Revolution. This revolution will create huge changes in the workforce, potentially displacing one-third of work activities while also creating entirely new job opportunities.

These broad changes have already begun. Most analysts agree that AI, automation, and digitalization have contributed significantly to the "hollowing out" of the American jobscape and the middle class by increasing the share of jobs at the high-paying and low-paying ends of the spectrum.

These new technologies may very well combine to create some of the most sweeping changes in the workplace that the world has ever seen. The number of people who are underemployed and unemployed may increase drastically, and the need for retraining will become paramount.

However, there is a third change occurring in the way we work: the rise of online and mobile platforms that allow peer-to-peer business opportunities, otherwise known as the "sharing economy."

Thank goodness for this timely trend, right?

If you are thinking that sharing economy gigs epitomized by companies like Uber and AirBNB could be your saving grace, think again. In the next chapter, we will take a look at the good, the bad, and the unprofitable side of the sharing economy in America.

CHAPTER 4

SHARING ECONOMY TO THE RESCUE?

"There will be growing pains along the way—and more horror stories, no doubt—but the sharing economy is here to stay."

-Glenn Carter, author of *Secrets of the Sharing Economy*[55]

I stayed at my first AirBNB rental in the fall of 2015, a "historic, downtown home" in Asheville, North Carolina with "sleek, uncluttered, minimalist decor" and hardwood floors. What's not to love about that, right? On a recent trip to New Orleans, my family used Ub-

[55] Goodreads. n.d. "Glenn Carter Quotes (Author of Secrets of the Sharing Economy) | Goodreads." Accessed April 20, 2018.
https://www.goodreads.com/author/quotes/14144978.Glenn_Carter.

er for 100 percent of our transportation around the city, learning a few choice tidbits about both New Orleans and Uber at the same time. I also happen to know a little about Uber because my brother drove for them for several years—more on that later.

AirBNB, Uber, Lyft, TaskRabbit, Upwork, Fiverr and scores more online workspaces like them are part of the burgeoning movement known as the sharing economy, which is allowing people to make money in a variety of ways, on the side or even in place of their day jobs.

The sharing economy is taking off worldwide, and it's poised to help you achieve your goal of an Independent Life!

Or is it?

Before dissecting the sharing economy to tease out its pros and cons, let's make sure we are on the same page with jargon. There are a lot of terms thrown around to describe trends in the way people are working. Here are some definitions and how I will use these terms:

Sole proprietor: The vast majority of people with small unincorporated businesses, more than 85 percent, are sole proprietorships or "solopreneurs," meaning they are the sole owners of an unincorporated business, which may or may not have employees.[56] Dan the Handyman, Sophie the Wildlife Artist, Nigel the Nature Tour Leader, and I are all examples of sole proprietorships.

Small business: The definition of a small business varies by agency. Generally, 500 or fewer employees is the Small Business Administration criterion, while HealthCare.gov defines small business as 50 or fewer employees, and the IRS considers a business with less than $10 million in assets small.[57] For our purposes, I use the term "small business" to mean one with 50 or fewer employees. Small businesses may be sole proprietorships, limited liability companies (LLCs), or corporations. All of the case studies featured in this book qualify as small businesses.

Self-employed: This is a broad term that means you work for yourself. This term includes sole proprietors, small businesses, and freelancers working via the sharing economy described below. It can also include incorporated businesses, but the majority of self-employed are unincorporated.[58]

---

[56] Hipple, Steven F., and Laurel A. Hammond. "Self-Employment in the United States : Spotlight on Statistics: U.S. Bureau of Labor Statistics." Accessed April 11, 2018. https://www.bls.gov/spotlight/2016/self-employment-in-the-united-states/home.htm.

[57] Bluemner, Adam. "How Does the Government Define 'Small Business'?" Software Connect, February 19, 2014. https://softwareconnect.com/blog/how-does-the-government-define-small-business/.

[58] Vilorio, Dennis. "Self-Employment: What to Know to Be Your Own Boss : Career Outlook: U.S. Bureau of Labor Statistics." United States Bureau of Labor Statistics. Accessed March 28, 2018. https://www.bls.gov/careeroutlook/2014/article/self-employment-what-to-know-to-be-your-own-boss.htm.

Entrepreneur: An entrepreneur is generally thought of as a special class of self-employed, one who creates something new (such as a startup) and also may take more of a personal risk in beginning the business than someone who puts out a shingle and begins providing a service.[59] Examples of entrepreneurs from our Independent Lifer case studies include José and Melanie the Sport Fishing Entrepreneurs and Maurrean the App Developer.

Nonemployer vs. employer: When people are self-employed and operate a small unincorporated business without employees, this is designated by the U.S. Census as a "non-employer."[60] My consulting business, Sophie the Wildlife Artist, and Dan the Handyman are all examples of nonemployer businesses, even though we may hire a subcontractor to assist with projects from time to time.

On the other hand, the Census defines businesses, often brick and mortar ones, that hire at least one other paid person, as employer businesses. Examples of employer businesses from our Independent Lifer case studies include Misha the Ballroom Studio Owner, Pam the Gym Owner, and Melanie and José the Sport Fishing Entrepreneurs.

---

[59] Seth, Shobhit. "Entrepreneurs and Entrepreneurship Defined." Investopedia, September 25, 2014. https://www.investopedia.com/articles/investing/092514/entrepreneur-vs-small-business-owner-defined.asp.

[60] U.S. Census. n.d. "Nonemployer Definitions." United States Census. Accessed March 28, 2018. https://www.census.gov/epcd/nonemployer/view/define.html.

Between 2003 and 2013, the U.S. Bureau of Labor Statistics reports that all industry sectors experienced growth in nonemployer businesses. These nonemployer businesses encompass a mix of work through both the sharing economy and the freelance economy, both described below. Between 2012 and 2022, the Bureau of Labor Statistics projects self-employment will grow in about half of all occupations.[61]

Sharing economy: The sharing economy is one that uses peer-to-peer networks to allow people to provide their services or products to a target market.[62] Most often this sharing economy is facilitated by one or more digital platforms that facilitate and profit from these peer-to-peer connections. The most well-known examples are AirBNB and Uber, but the number of platforms seems to be increasing weekly.

Freelancing/On-demand economy: Freelance or on-demand work can be providing skills, service, knowledge, or products—just about anything under the sun—for hire as an independent, whether you are a sole proprietor or LLC, and whether or not you have employees. Often the work transaction takes

[61] Torpey, Elka, and Andrew Hogan. "Working in a Gig Economy : Career Outlook: U.S. Bureau of Labor Statistics." Bureau of Labor Statistics. *Career Outlook* (blog), May 2016.
https://www.bls.gov/careeroutlook/2016/article/what-is-the-gig-economy.htm.

[62] Matofska, Benita. "What Is the Sharing Economy?" the people who share, 2016. http://www.thepeoplewhoshare.com/blog/what-is-the-sharing-economy/.

the form of a contract. My use of the term freelance economy in this book will describe those who work for themselves *without using a sharing platform.* However, most freelancers do not make this distinction themselves, and Upwork (a sharing platform) produces a major annual report based on a survey of freelancers in the U.S.

Gig: A gig describes a single task or chunk of work for which someone is hired, often but not always through a sharing platform or digital marketplace. Gig is a broad, generalist term that can mean almost any type of job, big or small, within the sharing and freelancing economies.

In fact, don't use the term gig economy! When comparing the terms "freelancing," "on demand," "sharing," and "gig" to describe the new worker economies, freelancers themselves prefer the term "freelance economy." "Gig economy" is their last choice, perhaps because it is so vague.[63]

Independent Lifer: Independent Lifer is the term I have coined to describe when you are self-employed (part of the freelance economy) or run a small employer business, make a good living, set your own rates, and assume 100 percent of the responsibility

---

[63] Upwork, Freelancers Union. "Freelancing in America: 2017 Survey - Upwork." Upwork, October 27, 2017. https://www.upwork.com/i/freelancing-in-america/2017/.

for your business operational decisions. In other words, you are truly your own boss.

The downside of "sharing"

The sharing economy is a blessing for many people because it has opened up new avenues for them to earn extra income in ways that were not possible just a few years ago. I love using AirBNB when I travel, meeting local people and experiencing each host's individual brand of hospitality.

However, if your goal is to build an Independent Life, you will want to think carefully about how the sharing economy can fit into those plans. There are several reasons for caution.

First, most sharing platforms take a cut of the income from every "gig" or transaction, above and beyond the cost of maintaining the platform. In some cases, this cut can be substantial.

For example, the rate paid by people to TaskRabbit includes a TaskRabbit service fee that is 15% of the total paid for the task, plus a 7.5 percent "Trust & Safety" fee that supports the platform.[64] This means taskers could make nearly 23 percent more if they were working directly with their clients. AirBNB gen-

---

[64] TaskRabbit, Inc. "What Is the TaskRabbit Service Fee?" TaskRabbit Support. Accessed March 28, 2018. http://support.taskrabbit.com/hc/en-us/articles/204411610-What-is-the-TaskRabbit-Service-Fee-.

erally takes a 3 percent booking fee directly from hosts and charges guests a roughly 20 percent service fee on top of the room rate (not including taxes or cleaning fees)[65].

Second, sharing platforms do not provide benefits equally to everyone. Those who are already affluent can charge the most for their Airbnb rentals in trendy neighborhoods, for example, and it has been argued that the sharing economy model is actually helping to divert money from traditional service workers (cab drivers, hotel workers) to more highly educated white collar workers. Much of this is probably not intentional, but rather a natural consequence of the way goods, education, and value are unevenly distributed in the world.[66]

Third, when you are dependent upon a third party platform for your customers and your pay, you have less control. You are, quite frankly, at their mercy.

The most notorious example

Let's take the most notorious example of this problem, one with which I'm familiar because my brother worked as an Uber driver from 2012 to 2015. My

---

[65] Airbnb, Inc. "What Are Airbnb Service Fees? | Airbnb Help Center." Airbnb, Inc. Accessed March 28, 2018.
https://www.airbnb.com/help/article/1857/what-are-airbnb-service-fees.
[66] Heller, Nathan. "Is the Gig Economy Working?" *The New Yorker*, May 8, 2017. https://www.newyorker.com/magazine/2017/05/15/is-the-gig-economy-working.

brother began his stint with Uber as a true fan, raving about his new-found freedom, which allowed him to choose his hours and make better money than he had in the restaurant industry. I listened as, over the course of several years, changes in the Uber business model began wearing away at his enthusiasm.

They began making changes where it really hurt: his wallet. My brother estimates that over that timeframe his pay rate dropped about 35 percent due to changes in the way that peak hours were defined as well as rate changes.

Since 2014, Uber has periodically decreased its prices for riders.[67] As you might expect, this means that Uber drivers are making less and less, with estimates of take home wages ranging from $8.77 to $4.54 per hour.[68] There is very little they can do about it.

If that is not discouraging enough, a 2017 study by Ridester[69] showed that, at the same time Uber has been effectively decreasing overall pay for their driv-

[67] O'Donovan, Caroline, and Jeremy Singer-Vine. "How Much Uber Drivers Actually Make Per Hour." BuzzFeed, June 22, 2016. https://www.buzzfeed.com/carolineodonovan/internal-uber-driver-pay-numbers.

[68] Dickey, Megan Rose. "How Much You Earn As An Uber Driver - Business Insider." *Business Insider*, June 28, 2014. http://www.businessinsider.com/how-much-you-earn-as-an-uber-driver-2014-6; Ridester Staff. "Uber Fees: How Much Does Uber ACTUALLY Take From Drivers?" Ridester. Accessed March 18, 2018. https://www.ridester.com/uber-fees/.

[69] Ridester Staff. "Uber Fees: How Much Does Uber ACTUALLY Take From Drivers?" Ridester. Accessed March 18, 2018. https://www.ridester.com/uber-fees/.

ers, the company is actually making significantly more than the 25 percent commission they advertise. This is because the rideshare companies take additional "booking" fees from riders, which are never even seen by the drivers.

Ridester found that an Uber commission could go as high as 42.75 percent for a minimum fare ride in San Francisco. Analyzing 37 actual UberX trips in San Francisco, they found the median commission was 39 percent. That means for an $8.03 fare, the driver would receive $5.08.[70]

In short, drivers are now having to drive more time to make the same money that they did several years ago. To earn $10 in 2013, a driver had to travel 2.36 miles (in San Francisco), whereas in 2016 that distance has doubled to 4.71 miles. In addition, Uber drivers must absorb not only the costs of fuel, but other charges such as "municipal tolls, airport surcharges, or processing fees for split payments," and the long-term costs of maintenance for their heavily used vehicles.[71]

My own view is that sharing economy gigs are best used as a supplement to your main source of income or potentially as an effective stepping stone toward

[70] Ridester Staff. "Uber Fees: How Much Does Uber ACTUALLY Take From Drivers?" Ridester. Accessed March 18, 2018. https://www.ridester.com/uber-fees/.

[71] Uber. "Legal | Uber." United States. Uber, 2018. https://www.uber.com/legal/terms/us/.

an Independent Life, but relying on the sharing economy for your living is probably not a good long-term strategy.

Wages without benefits and the "precariat"

Look at it this way: when you use a sharing platform, you may legally be considered an independent contractor, but the main benefit you have in common with a self-employed freelancer or small business owner is the ability to pick your hours. Otherwise, your situation is not unlike working for a company and giving them roughly 20 to 30 percent of your salary in return for zero benefits—usually no health insurance, no retirement, no vacation, and no sick leave.

No reimbursement for out-of-pocket expenses in most cases (such as car maintenance, cost of power, and internet to run your computer, etc.). Oh yes, and if you are working 30 hours or more per week (in most cases) no unemployment either if for some reason you can't work (although this applies to independent freelancers as well)[72]. In some cases, however, sharing platforms do cover the cost of insurance, and as an Independent Lifer you probably would need to provide that insurance for yourself as well.

---

[72] Rideshare Dashboard. 2014. "Can Lyft or Uber Drivers Claim Unemployment?" Rideshare Dashboard (blog). December 25, 2014. https://medium.com/@RideshareDash/can-lyft-or-uber-drivers-claim-unemployment-e67efa688b89.

The company is sometimes even setting your fee for you, while taking a significant cut of each transaction. Some critics are starting to point out that many of the jobs created by digital sharing work platforms do not add up to a living wage[73], while others point out that the larger the sharing network, the more attractive it is to customers, creating monopolies[74].

Above all, you have no control over the decisions that the sharing platform makes, which could significantly impact your business.

There is even a word that has begun cropping up more frequently within the paragraphs of business magazines in recent years, which describes the class of people who are stuck in endless low-pay jobs with little security: the precariat. Precariat is a term that combines the words precarious with proletariat.

The hallmarks of the precariat, according to the labor economist who coined the term, are "unstable" labor conditions, lack of a cohesive identity within society, and lack of security.[75]

---

[73] Lund, Susan. "What the Rise of the Freelance Economy Means for the Future of Work." *Huffington Post*, October 30, 2015. https://www.huffingtonpost.com/susan-lund/freelance-economy-future-work_b_8420866.html

[74] Smith, N. Craig. "Who's Responsible? The Ethics of the Sharing Economy | Alliance for Research on Corporate Sustainability." Alliance for Research on Corporate Sustainability. Accessed March 18, 2018. https://corporate-sustainability.org/whos-responsible-the-ethics-of-the-sharing-economy/.

[75] Standing, Guy. "Meet the Precariat, the New Global Class Fueling the Rise of Populism." World Economic Forum, November 9, 2016. https://www.weforum.org/agenda/2016/11/precariat-global-class-rise-of-populism/.

I'm a champion of self-employment, but if you are forever dependent on relatively low-paying peer-to-peer platforms as the sole or primary source of your income, I'm afraid you may be next in line to join the precariat.

As an Independent Lifer, on the other hand, while you cannot control the decisions that your clients or customers make, you have far more control over your business. You can be creative and work hard to find and retain customers. You set your own fees, taking into account the need to plan for health insurance, those days when you're down with the flu, family beach trips, and your eventual golden years.

The main benefit that sharing/peer-to-peer platforms have over self-employment is they provide immediate access to a potentially huge, and seemingly inexhaustible market. However, don't make the mistake of assuming that all platforms that provide access to a wider market for your talents necessarily follow this model!

Other types of online work platforms have begun cropping up, which act more like a service provider to an entrepreneur. For example, NearMe provides anyone with the ability to set up their own peer-to-peer platform for economic exchanges, but they charge only a setup fee and monthly hosting fee with support, without taking a percentage of each transaction.[76]

Furthermore, just wait a few years! There is much hope and speculation that blockchain technology may finally topple the dominance of current online sharing platforms by making direct transactions between individuals the world over more feasible.[77]

Here's a question of the utmost importance to ask yourself: *Is it worth putting in the extra time and effort now—along with accepting a potential loss of income in the early stages while building your own clientele—so that you can create the capacity to gain a higher income and greater security over the long term?*

Best use of the sharing economy

Sharing platforms can be wonderful as side hustles to help you earn extra cash and save money for your eventual transition to an Independent Life (a key step I'll cover in Chapter 6). They also create a great chance to test the waters, giving you a sense of how much you like working for yourself and whether the Independent Life might be for you. Finally, your work

---

[76] Ignaczak, Nina Misuraca. "3 Platforms to Start Your Own Sharing Service." Shareable, April 22, 2014. https://www.shareable.net/blog/3-platforms-to-start-your-own-sharing-service.

[77] Filippi, Primavera De. "What Blockchain Means for the Sharing Economy." Harvard Business Review, March 15, 2017. https://hbr.org/2017/03/what-blockchain-means-for-the-sharing-economy.

through the sharing economy may be able to serve as your entree into full-time work in the same or a related field.

I used several "content mill" writing platforms to earn a little extra cash before I became a full-time free-lancer. While I did not earn much money, I learned how they work, I learned more about the topics that I chose to research, and I learned how writing for the web is different from other writing.

Although I could not support myself that way, I gained a small platform to increase my exposure. I shared my best articles online on my LinkedIn CV before I even had my own website. Those articles showed I was still current and still "in the game."

As long as you are careful not to violate your contract with whatever company has contracted with you, some peer-to-peer sharing platforms may also serve as an apprenticeship for the real thing: running a similar business full-time. I am not advocating violating peer-to-peer contractual arrangements, but online "piecework" or providing concierge services through sharing platforms may in some cases provide a good foundational work experience for you. You can put it on your resume, but more importantly, you can use the experience and learning to transition to a similar business in your Independent Life.

Summary

The sharing economy, characterized by peer-to-peer platforms such as TaskRabbit and Lyft, is transforming business in America and around the world. Working these kinds of gigs may provide a great supplemental income and help you save for the day when you go Independent.

Beware, however, the idea that sharing platforms could form the basis of a sustainable independent career. For that, I believe it's far better to plan for your own business.

But do you have what it takes to run your own business, and how can you find your niche? That's what Part II of this book is all about.

PART II

BUILDING
AN INDEPENDENT LIFE:
THE HOW OF
SELF-EMPLOYMENT

CHAPTER 5

WHAT DOES IT TAKE TO GO IN-DEPENDENT?

"People are now, more than ever before, aware of the careers that they're not pursuing."

- Kathryn Minshew, the CEO of the Muse, a job search and career advice site[78]

With her long, wavy hair the color of a sandy beach, her down-to-earth personality, her quick smile, and her lifelong pursuit of twin passions for art and nature, Sophie is a poster child for the Independent Lifer. For the whole of her career, Sophie has worked

---

[78] Heller, Nathan. "Is the Gig Economy Working?" The New Yorker, May 8, 2017. https://www.newyorker.com/magazine/2017/05/15/is-the-gig-economy-working.

for herself or on contract. Here's her take on why she chose this path.

"I'm free to decide what I'm going to work on, what I'm going to paint or write or draw. Having that independence and ability to set your own schedule is the best. It's also the hardest thing, too, because sometimes it's hard to keep yourself disciplined."

If you have reservations about whether or not entrepreneurship is for you, this chapter will help you consider that question. With the ongoing decline of corporate jobs in America; pressures of artificial intelligence, automation, and digitalization; and the risks associated with the sharing economy, the opportunities for self-employment will only increase. I believe it's essential to think about this and prepare.

In fact, jobageddon may already be here, only it's taking the form of a mass movement to self-employment! The *FreshBooks Second Annual Self-employment Report* found that the U.S. workforce is currently undergoing a dramatic shift: away from corporate employment toward self-employment. The number of self-employed in the U.S. could triple by the year 2020. As the founder of FreshBooks states,

"Whether or not change occurs at this pace, it's clear the mindset of the American worker has shifted."[79]

All of the people I interviewed as case studies for this book agree on the list of four traits I am about to share with you, which provide an essential foundation for success as an Independent Lifer. These traits are passion, a good work ethic, a modicum of people skills, and courage.

Passion

What is passion? The dictionary defines it as "a strong and barely controllable emotion." What's emotion got to do with business? Everything, as it turns out. Passion is the motivator that drives people to achieve a goal because they care deeply about the results of what they are doing.

Try this exercise: notice people in your day-to-day life who work for themselves. It may be a brick-and-mortar business, such as your hairdresser or a boutique clothing store, or it may be a freelancer who works for a variety of clients from home. Notice the people you have a chance to hire or transact business with who are likely self-employed: your doctor,

[79] FreshBooks. "New FreshBooks Report Reveals Millennials as Catalysts Behind Self-Employment Movement, Opting for More Autonomy | FreshBooks." FreshBooks, February 21, 2018. https://www.freshbooks.com/press/releases/new-freshbooks-report-reveals-millennials-as-catalysts-behind-self-employment-movement-opting-for-more-autonomy.

your dentist, writers or designers who interact with you in your work place, your accountant, your favorite local musician. Perhaps you have friends who have already made the jump.

Ask them why they do what they do. I guarantee in almost every case their answer is going to reveal what they are passionate about: helping people to stay well, to connect, or to feel good about themselves; creative self-expression; fascination and focus on a very specific topic; working to make the world a better place.

Corey, who works as a freelance Financial Services advisor unaffiliated with any single insurance company or investment firm, works 100 percent for himself because his passion is to do right by his clients. "The reality is you can't truly be unbiased if you are affiliated with one company. There will be quotas. My ultimate loyalty is to my customer, but if I work for someone else it's the company that comes first."

When their energy runs out, when things are not going well, when they have a negative interaction with someone in their lives, passion is what allows Independent Lifers to bounce back just as strong as before. Passion is what allows you to refill the well, time and again.

Passion is also what drives you to succeed because passion makes you naturally interested in keeping up with changing practices and the state of knowledge in your field. Why? Because you find it inherently interesting! You *want* to know. And also because you want to keep your competitive edge.

An essential ingredient of passion, in my book, is the ability to see yourself as part of a grander whole. What you are doing is stretching yourself to your fullest potential to make a difference in the world.

Your niche may be small—let's face it, with more than seven billion people in the world (and that statistic will date this book more quickly than any other), just about everyone's niche is small, relative to the whole. But small does not mean insignificant. We are talking about someone's *life*—your life—what could be more significant than that?

I'll be honest. What I do from one day to the next is not earth-shattering in importance. I plan, develop, and provide communications for a variety of clients. This includes things like interviewing, writing, research, electronic newsletters, social media, webinars, analyses of web-based analytics, and strategic planning. Sounds pretty commonplace, doesn't it? Perhaps even downright boring to some of you. But here is the key for me: I provide communications in support of biodiversity and natural resource conservation.

Since a very young age, the natural world has been a source of wonder, beauty, and communion with something greater than myself that has inspired in me both awe and a sense of peace. When I am putting together a newsletter about Eastern Hellbenders or running a webinar about the latest research on oyster beds or writing a strategy that will help conservation organizations reach private landowners, I not only find it interesting, I find it of utmost importance. I see my connection to something much bigger.

I've found my passion. I can't recommend it highly enough.

You may already know what your passion is, in which case, you are ahead of the game. Maurrean the App Developer sees passion as essential, but she believes it could be passion for your business or passion for what your business income allows you to do.

"I think of life as a chess game. You've got some kind of talent and you've got abilities. The first thing you have to figure out is what are your chess pieces—your great ability, your talent for selling, whatever it may be—and how to use those pieces to create the future that you want."

But don't worry if you're scratching your head right now. There is a tested method for finding one's passion!

Steve Kotler, a New York Times best-selling business author, has a five-step method that he says works for anyone who is wondering what their passion is. Kotler discusses passion this way:

"[W]hy is passion important? Simple. It's a profound focusing mechanism. We pay more attention to those things we believe in . . . But focused attention is the ultimate gateway drug. It drives performance, it increases productivity, and it triggers flow (which, in turn, further increases performance and productivity)."[80]

Here is a summary of Kotler's five-step method for finding your passion:

Step One: Make A List

Make a list of 25 things you're curious about (using pen and paper is better than using the computer). Be specific and choose things that you are willing to spend your free time investigating.

Step Two: Hunt for Intersections

Find places where your 25 ideas intersect. Make a venn diagram or a mind map or just use your imagination to find those connections. This step is essen-

---

[80] Kotler, Steven. "The Passion Recipe: Four Steps To Total Fulfillment." *Forbes*, March 27, 2015.
https://www.forbes.com/sites/stevenkotler/2015/03/27/the-passion-recipe-four-steps-to-total-fulfillment/.

tial because Kotler says, "When multiple curiosity streams intersect you create the necessary conditions for pattern recognition, which is the linking of ideas together. Humans love pattern recognition. Whenever we recognize a pattern, the brain releases a tiny squirt of the neurochemical dopamine and, for cultivating passion, this is a very big deal. Dopamine increases focus, increases pattern recognition (feedback loop), feel-good drug."

José, the Sport Fishing Entrepreneur, was able to bring together many of his overlapping interests by focusing on the well-accepted conservation approach of local community involvement in natural resource enterprises, combined with his love of all things marine. When he discovered the demand for sport fishing in the waters around the tiny island of Cedros, off the Pacific coast of Baja Mexico, he put the three together, helping tourists to enjoy a sea fishing experience that also provides economic benefits to Cedros islanders.

Step Three: Play

Spend time every day focusing on your overlapping interests. Kotler recommends spending 10 to 20 minutes a day learning more, and in our information rich world that will not be hard to do. It's important to feed your curiosities on a daily basis.

Again, why is daily important? "When you advance your knowledge a little bit at a time, you're giving your subconscious a chance to process that information. . . .

"Once you have learned enough to organize the history of a field into a little story, that story will lock into place. This gives you a structural framework to attach new facts to." Having this story makes it much easier for you to remember new facts; you'll learn faster and begin developing expertise.

Step Four: Go Public

Once you have developed a certain level of knowledge and expertise, you can begin adding something substantive to the dialogues that are going on out there all the time. By learning, playing, then going public—possibly through one of those online sharing platforms—you will begin getting valuable feedback from others about your ideas. You may also begin to build a community of individuals with common interests.

Step Five: Turn Passion Into Purpose

This is the critical step that will allow you to go from high energy and interest to a useful business idea. Make another list, only this time make it about 15 huge problems for the world that you would like to help solve. As Kotler says, "[T]he world's biggest problems are the world's biggest business opportunities."[81]

Next, look for places where your passion intersects with an issue far bigger than yourself. That linkage is your purpose. You have found the keyhole through which your individual interests, talents, and efforts (your passion!) can translate into making a broader difference for the planet and in people's lives.

<u>There's yet another step . . .</u>

To translate your passion into a viable business, I believe there is a sixth step to this method: You need to find the magic carpet that will take you through your keyhole of interest into the wider world.

I have found that it's useful to think about the skills and tasks that you enjoy and are good at (usually there's significant overlap between the two) rather than entire jobs or businesses. In other words, once you find your passion and your purpose, the next fundamental question is, "What will you/your business do to meet that need?"

I'll use myself as an example. Natural resource management and biodiversity conservation is a huge field. That's my passion, but how do I fit into that?

---

[81] Kotler, Steven. "The Passion Recipe: Four Steps To Total Fulfillment." Forbes, March 27, 2015.
https://www.forbes.com/sites/stevenkotler/2015/03/27/the-passion-recipe-four-steps-to-total-fulfillment/.

In college, I had to select a major (biology), and then I had to decide if I would go on to become a research scientist or something else. I discovered I did not have the patience for scientific research. It can be a years-long process to answer one question that advances understanding in your field. I wanted to see concrete results more rapidly.

I held a series of jobs that taught me a huge amount about the "conservation culture" in America. I developed the story in my head that Kotler talks about: how conservation works in our country. Factoids that were important began fitting into the framework and sticking more easily.

As for skills, all of my jobs required some level of writing: grant proposals, syntheses of scientific research and expert viewpoints, write-ups of interviews, etc. I slowly began to take more interest in the craft of writing. Eventually, that craft (along with my knowledge of conservation) was the skill around which I was able to build my business. I also discovered that I really enjoy interviewing people (and am pretty good at it—which comes first?). So communications is the magic carpet that has taken me through my keyhole of passion for the natural world into a business that makes a contribution to conservation.

Another resource that contains many valuable insights about discovering what is meaningful and interesting to you is the book, *Dream Job: Redefined* by Mitch Matthews.[82] Although this book focuses on jobs, many of the exercises for figuring out what you want to do with your life apply equally well to someone with a goal of self-employment.

Work ethic

No question, if you are going to work for yourself, you have to be willing and able to work hard. What does that mean? It means that you will need to be able to do each of the following as you are building and running your business.

Be self-motivated. No one is telling you when you have to report to work or setting your deadlines. There will be no reprimands if things don't get done, and there will be no inspirational speakers to inspire you (unless you seek them out yourself). Work gets done because you do it, and it happens in the timeframe that you set (or negotiate with your client).

Ivan the Cinematographer tells a story from his teenage years about self-discipline. His mother implemented an organizational process at her company based on the system described in the book *Getting*

---

[82] Matthews, Mitch. 2018. *Dream Job: Redefined: The New Rules for Creating a Career That Matters and Doing Work You Love.* MMJM Companies, Incorporated.

Things Done by David Allen[83]. "It's a system of information processing and focusing on what's important rather than urgent. It's about knowing where you want to get, ditching the 'fat' of your day, and just doing the stuff that gets you there. That book gave me the discipline I needed, and my mom inspired me to read it."

Being self-disciplined is a natural outgrowth of self-motivation. Self-discipline includes:

- setting deadlines for yourself and meeting them
- arriving on time to your appointments (whether meeting in-person, online, or over the phone)
- having pride in the quality of your work
- avoiding procrastination on the tasks that you don't enjoy that much (there will always be a few)
- being willing to put in long hours, when necessary, and go the extra mile

To succeed at your own business, once your passion has led you to your "niche" (i.e. the specific and unique blend of services/products you offer), you have to deliver! Your service and/or product needs to

---

[83] Allen, David. 2002. Getting Things Done: The Art of Stress-Free Productivity: David Allen: 9780142000281: Amazon.Com: Books. Penguin Books. https://www.amazon.com/Getting-Things-Done-Stress-Free-Productivity/dp/0142000280.

be of high quality and value, otherwise you will not be able to build a clientele or customer base. There will almost always be other places they can go for a similar product. Even if your niche is truly unique, people will forego what you offer if they don't think it's worth the price tag.

People skills

This one is tricky for some people. I am not saying that to be successful with your own enterprise, you have to be a people-loving, outgoing extrovert. I'm not saying you have to be able to sell wool to Hawaiians. I am saying you have to have a certain level of emotional intelligence.

This means, basically, that you know how to be *nice*. You treat people courteously. If you say, "I'll get back to you by Thursday," you do so. You listen well to everyone, and especially to your clients or potential clients (making strategic use of reflecting back your understanding about important conversations). As you are developing or creating your service or product, you solicit your customers' feedback, and you respond to it.

You may be providing a "turn-key" service, such as Dan the Handyman, who is 100 percent responsible for refinishing a bathroom when he takes on a project. You may be providing an essential component of a much greater whole, such as many of the communications products I develop for my clients.

In both cases, you should approach your relationship with your client as a partnership because they will be the ones making the ultimate call on whether or not you did a good job. The partnership relationship creates a feedback loop, in which you can respond to the concerns, ideas, and perspectives of your customers, which means their needs will be met.

Another aspect of emotional intelligence is how you handle conflict. There will be difficult moments when you receive feedback that is painful. This is where that expression "the customer is always right" comes from. Even though this may not always be technically true, you need to keep that in mind when your favorite idea is being tossed onto the garbage heap, your advice as the expert is being overruled, your customers' demands are unreasonable, or the results of your work are deemed unacceptable.

This is not just a matter of stoically taking the criticism. It's a matter of interacting with your client or customer to ensure that you really understand his or her concerns, and then a willingness to go back to the drawing board to make your product or your next service better.

Pam the Gym Owner says, "I don't believe the customer is always right, but the customer always has a right to be respected and heard." Pam is emphatic on this point.

Constructive criticism from a client is pure gold. Sometimes you will not get much feedback, and you'll need to ask for it. This is an effective practice whether your client is happy or dissatisfied with your work.

Think about it. Say you hired someone to wash your car, they did a crappy job, and you paid them and let it go. Without asking for your feedback, they'll walk away happy, but you will never hire them again.

On the other hand, if you pointed out to them the places they were missing, and they responded by improving their performance and left you with a spic and span vehicle, you'd be happy to hire them again. Not only did they do a good job, but they listened to you, plus now you know their work, and they understand your standards.

When you are in business for yourself, it's your baby, and you'll want to improve. The best way to do that, beyond further training to improve your own skills, is to attend to the feedback you receive: the good, the bad, and the unsolicited. We are all individuals with unique viewpoints. You can learn a lot about how to broaden your appeal to future clients by learning from the feedback that each one gives you along the way.

Emotional intelligence also means knowing how to handle anger as well. It means that when something big or small ticks you off, you know how to let off steam and cool down before approaching the situation again.

In the almost 10 years I've been in business, I have had only one situation in which a client and I had a heated exchange. If I could do a "retake" of that episode I would have suggested—as soon as I realized that our disagreement was escalating—that we discuss the issue at a later time. But the reality is, life is not a dress rehearsal. We don't get retakes, but we can learn from our mistakes.

Courage

This last quality was not on my original list of essential elements for success in building an Independent Life. I never thought of myself as courageous, just at the end of my rope. However, several of the people I interviewed pointed this out.

Maurrean the App Developer also points out that sometimes a dose of desperation, rather than courage, might boost your ability to risk going independent! I know in my case that was certainly true.

My hairdresser in Memphis, Tennessee runs a hair studio that Salon magazine has ranked among the top 200 in the country for the past several years. She agrees that running a business takes a degree of courage: first, to take the leap and work for yourself, but then to continually do what needs to be done. That means making the sometimes painful changes and adjustments that are required to make your business successful.

It's often said that courage is not an absence of fear but the ability to take action in the face of that fear. The courage of an entrepreneur is the ability to take calculated risks aimed at success while staring down the fear of failure.

Researchers who study entrepreneurs have focused on this tolerance for risk. It is widely accepted that people who are risk-averse are less likely to become entrepreneurs, but, as we shall see in Chapter 6, it may be that risk aversion is more likely to influence how rather than if people start new businesses.[84]

Summary

It takes passion, a great work ethic, people skills, and courage (or desperation) to begin and to run your own business. Our Independent Lifers agree on these points.

---

[84] Raffiee, Joseph, and Jie Feng. "Should I Quit My Day Job?: A Hybrid Path to Entrepreneurship." Academy of Management Journal 57, no. 4 (August 1, 2014): 936–63. https://doi.org/10.5465/amj.2012.0522.

Passion will give you a virtually inexhaustible well of interest in what you do and the desire to excel. The work ethic will make it possible for you to set realistic goals and do what it takes to achieve them. A degree of people skills and emotional intelligence is necessary to facilitate your interactions with clients and customers, although this does not mean you have to be a "life of the party" type of person. Finally, courage is required to make the leap, take calculated risks, and generally to embrace change.

The question for many of us who may have held traditional jobs for years if not decades is: how does one make the switch from employee to employer, especially in mid-career? Chapter 6 will answer this question. You'll also learn how several Independent Lifers successfully navigated their switch at mid-career.

CHAPTER 6

MAKING THE MID-LIFE CAREER SWITCH

"Twenty years from now, you will be more disappointed by the things that you didn't do than by the ones you did do. So throw off the bowlines. Sail away from the safe harbor. Catch the trade winds in your sails. Explore. Dream. Discover."

-H. Jackson Brown's mother, in the book
P.S. I Love You[85]

You already have years of experience and are considering a mid-career switch to self-employment. You know yourself, your skills, and you firmly believe you have the ability to achieve more.

---

[85] Brown, Jr., H. Jackson. 1991. *P.S. I Love You: When Mom Wrote, She Always Saved the Best for Last.* Rutledge Hill Pr.

If you are in the middle of your career, ready to switch tracks and build toward an Independent Life, there is good news and there is bad news.

The bad news

First, the bad news: you've got a ton of competition, and it's only going to increase over time. The ranks of full-time self-employed professionals are on track to triple by the year 2020.[86] Furthermore, that competition is increasingly going to come from millennials and the generations that follow them, who because they are at the beginning of their careers may be willing and able to work for less than someone with a longer work history and/or a family.

Finally, the millennial component of your competition are "digital natives." Having grown up with an iPhone in their hands, they are eager and able to take advantage of the exploding number of digital applications and services filling the online workspace.

The good news

Now, here's the good news—and there is a lot of it! As a mid-career switcher, you have years of experience, which confer some powerful advantages:

---

[86] Moulton, Cary, and Dave Cosgrave. "Second Annual Self-Employment Report." Freshbooks cloud accounting, February 21, 2018. https://www.freshbooks.com/_themes/freshbooks/brand-assets/2018selfemploymentreport.pdf.

1) Experience translates into a degree of expertise in your field, with skills and knowledge earned in the workplace for which there is no substitute.

2) Time spent in the workplace means by now you are likely to have more realistic ideas about what you are good at, and you are more likely to understand where your true passions lie.

3) Through your years of work, you have developed a network of colleagues, supervisors, and friends who may prove helpful in finding your first clients or customers.

4) Having worked for a while, you may have some savings that can be used to invest in your business or as an income cushion when you are starting out.

5) There is an age where money is everything—when you have a family with kids to support. On the other hand, you may well be beyond this stage, in which case you could be more flexible and willing to accept a lower income to get your business off the ground than someone with a family to support.

6) Rightly or wrongly, there is a perception among some people that older workers have a better work ethic than Millennials.

7) Above all, if you still have a job, you have the opportunity to take advantage of what researchers call hybrid entrepreneurship.

Hybrid entrepreneurship

Hybrid entrepreneurship is the process of starting a business while retaining your "day job" in an existing organization. Whereas the conventional wisdom until recently has been that a business is more likely to succeed when the entrepreneur can devote 100 percent of his or her time to the new venture, recent research casts doubt on this idea.

A 2014 study based on data from 1994 to 2008 about 5,299 individuals found that "the hazard of exit is 33.3 percent lower for individuals who enter full-time self-employment in a staged process relative to those who enter directly from paid work."[87] Translation: hybrid entrepreneurs who keep their day job and begin self-employment part-time have much higher survival rates relative to those who quit their day job to begin a new venture.

In fact, although I did not think of myself this way at the time, I was a hybrid entrepreneur while working as a teacher. I did some freelance writing developing web content in my field, natural resource conservation. I began working as a hybrid without any intention of ever making it full-time work, and yet eventually that is what happened!

---

[87] Raffiee, Joseph, and Jie Feng. "Should I Quit My Day Job?: A Hybrid Path to Entrepreneurship." *Academy of Management Journal* 57, no. 4 (August 1, 2014): 936–63. https://doi.org/10.5465/amj.2012.0522.

In today's society, where most people will change jobs 10 to 15 times before they "retire,"[88] the hybrid route to the Independent Life is becoming more and more common. What follows are four stories from five Independent Lifers detailing how they began their full-time businesses using the hybrid model.

A word of caution

While entrepreneurs tend to love what they do, it's important to be realistic. Many of the Independent Lifers interviewed for this book cautioned about the temptation to take what you love to do to relax and turn it into work. It can be done, but be aware if you do so.

Nigel the Nature Tour Leader says, "I'm working all the time, it never ends. I work on weekends and almost every day, sixteen hours a day sometimes. It's because I want to do it. But sometimes it would be nice to have somebody else do some of my tasks for a change." Nigel also cautions not to turn your passion into an obsession, which is a clear route to burnout.

As my father always used to say, "There is a reason why they call it work!" Will you still love it? Yes. Will

---

[88] Doyle, Alison. "How Often Do People Change Jobs?" The Balance. Accessed March 19, 2018. https://www.thebalance.com/how-often-do-people-change-jobs-2060467.

you sometimes get tired of it? Absolutely. Will it still be the thing you turn to for relaxation? Probably not.

José & Melanie the Sport Fishing Entrepreneurs

Cedros Outdoor Adventures is an example of how a sole (or in this case "couple") proprietorship grew into a business supporting upwards of 20 employees, a fleet of fishing pangas, and a hand-crafted lodge with a breathtaking view of the Pacific. But the creation of this sport fishing company was not the result of a well-thought-out business plan. The concept grew organically out of a period of trial and error.

Soon after their marriage in 2007, Melanie and José both found themselves out of work. Whereas Melanie had tried, and largely failed, to move her photography business from Virginia to California, José had lost his job with a conservation nonprofit working in Baja. All of this occurred at the height of the Great Recession, when everyone was tightening their purse strings.

A nature photographer as well as a marine biologist, José tried to make a go of selling nature postcards, while Melanie continued to pursue wedding photography clients in the highly competitive San Diego area.

"We had five micro-businesses at one time, just to get cash here and there," Melanie sighs. One of their microbusinesses was ecotours to Cedros island, 270 miles to the south of Ensenada in the Pacific Ocean.

José had experience with the well-accepted conservation approach of local community involvement to ensure people have a stake in the stewardship of their natural resources. José is a true thalassophile—someone who loves everything about the ocean. He wanted to create an ecotours business that would help people experience the seals, dolphins, sea lions, pelicans, frigatebirds, fish, and other abundant marine life around the remote island while also providing economic benefits to Cedros islanders.

Working with a partner who grew up on the island, José quickly discovered that ecotours did not attract much interest; however, he noticed scores of people with fancy fishing gear tooling the waters around the island in long-range boats from San Diego. But those fishermen never seemed to dock at Cedros at all, much less contribute to the local economy of the island.

José got the idea to start sport fishing tours that included spending time on the island, which would allow fishers to skip the grueling same-day return journey to San Diego by boat. In 2008, José and Melanie began flying people to Cedros, using the only local hotel to put people up, and using boats (pangas) rented from the local fishing co-op to take people out angling.

"We were working in an area with no infrastructure whatsoever for tourism or sport fishing. We had about 10 people come our first year," Melanie explains with a note of humor in her voice. "That was okay because we were learning our way, everything was brand new.

"At that time, people were also nervous about going to Mexico, and the economy was still bad. In retrospect, it all worked out perfectly because as the economy recovered, our business grew with it. We grew slowly enough to figure out how to create this whole new enterprise."

Maurrean the App Developer

Maurrean is in the process of reinventing herself for at least the third time in her life. The first time happened over a lengthy timespan, as Maurrean clawed her way out of a small, rural town in Arkansas, eventually earning a college degree that allowed her to put her considerable creativity to use. "I was a freelancer in college, designing publications and logos for the University of Tennessee and others. Then I went to work in corporate America: at a travel agency, advertising agencies, and other random companies."

The second time she was forced to reinvent herself came after her husband of nine years and the father of her two daughters drowned in a tragic kayaking accident. Maurrean eventually sold the small, but highly regarded digital marketing company that she had run with her husband in Memphis, TN during the course of their nine-year marriage.

She decided to go after her own clients, establishing a project management consultancy focused on digital marketing and the sometimes cloak-and-dagger field of competitor research. She had already successfully managed several projects for smart phone and web-site apps. But this case study is not about Maurrean's consulting business.

As she tells it, "In that segment of my life, I had a decent income. I only had to work 15 hours per week to the pay bills, and I had a lot of time. My girls are teenagers and didn't need me a lot. I had been looking for something to be passionate about."

Maurrean's third time of reinvention arrived in 2016—in the form of a lawn care specialist dispatched to her house to manage her weeds. The tech came to her house, sprayed her grass, and did a really good job. "He knew his product, knew his weeds, and explained that no amount of herbicide was going to kill my unwanted weeds because they were bulb plants."

"I could see he was implementing his corporate training. He gave great customer service, and I wanted to give him a recommendation, so he would not always be spraying grass. I wanted to improve his chances. That's when I realized I really had no options for doing that beyond calling his boss, in which case my recommendation was not going to stick with him past that job.

"How ludicrous that we, as citizens of the internet, can post recommendations online for professionals via LinkedIn, but not for the segment of the population that really needs it! It seems if you're not a 'knowledge' worker, you're not allowed to have that."

This was the seed of Maurrean's idea. She thought there must be a way for bank tellers and plumbers to create online profiles that showcase their transferable skills. She wanted to create an app that would allow her and other customers to give an impressive recommendation to her lawn care tech that could follow him throughout his career.

Maurrean discussed the idea with various people and at one point, she decided to give up. But the idea had her in its clutches and simply would not let go. She finally seized an opportunity by presenting her idea to an investor whom she knew professionally.

When he gave her the green light, AlwaysPro.co was born. AlwaysPro is to working class professionals what LinkedIn is to those with a bachelor's degree or higher.

Maurrean eventually received startup cash from two investors, and she has spent a good deal of her own money to get through the startup phase. She applied and in May of 2017 was admitted into StartCo incubator system, a program in Memphis that mentors the founders of technology-based startup companies. Out of a total 300 applicants, 17 were admitted, and she was one of 14 able to complete the program.

"The program concentrates on marketing because everybody needs it. Precisely because that was my background, I got overwhelmed by all the possibilities. To be able to focus and prune back on those ideas was very helpful. StartCo also put me in contact with a lot of people and introduced me to two of the people currently on my board of advisors."

While launching AlwaysPro.co, Maurrean spoke with over 50 hiring managers and recruiters. She learned that AlwaysPro could serve as a bridge between job recruiters and good, hard-working people who don't always know how to present themselves.

"For recruiters, experience is rarely the issue. Some popular resume sites that are already out there provide a horrible showcase: they are simply black ink on a white page, saying 'here's what I did.' Instead, recruiters want to know about your soft skills: How will you interact with people? Do you know how to be polite? AlwaysPro is that bridge to allow personal testimonials on the basis of actual customer interactions."

Maurrean learned through experimentation, as well as talking to people who represent her market, that AlwaysPro could provide another related service that would be far more profitable and require less work. "That's called a pivot," says Maurrean. "Our focus has switched from a service tech market to one of the students coming out of two-year college programs." That way, her app will serve a very similar set of customers *before* they enter the job market.

Dan the Handyman

Dan, whom you first met in Chapter 2 after he was summarily canned from his engineering job upon returning from vacation, was 57 when that happened. He didn't have a plan down on paper, but in the back of his mind, he had been contemplating his next move for some time.

"While I was working as an Engineering Manager for that company, I anticipated that I would not work there the rest of my life." There was too much turmoil, and in the four and a half years Dan was there, his immediate manager changed three times.

When Dan lost his job, he was making six figures and had been divorced for about six years, with his children grown and raising their own families. Throughout his time at the company, "I banked every dime I could and lived under my means. I saved my butt off—saved, saved, saved!

"I had a nice house (but nothing extravagant) in a nice area, that I'd bought as a fixer-upper. I bought it for $165,000 and now it's worth $212,000. I splurged on my truck because that's what I really wanted, but it was my only luxury. I paid for it in cash. I also maxed out my 401K savings, and put in the additional 10 percent 'catchup contribution' for folks over 55. The question had already been planted in my mind: when this job ends, will I want to go back to doing this again?

"When I did get let go, I got a healthy three months' severance, went on unemployment, and was debt-free with the exception of my mortgage," Dan says evenly. "I thought, shoot I can wash dishes and make $1,100 per month for the house payment!"

Dan had set himself up for being able to go out and "do something" on his own.

When Dan realized that he did not want to go back to a corporate job, he was assaulted by questions. What about retirement? How to live? Will I have to sell my house? What would I do?

He weighed buying into a new type of business versus doing what he already knew: construction and how to fix things. Then came the $64,000 question: "How do I do it and how do I get started and let people know about my business?"

It just so happened that Dan was a member on the Nextdoor social website for neighborhoods, and in August of 2016, a retired school teacher was trying to find someone to remodel his master bathroom. He was asking because most contractors would not do such a small job.

Dan thought, "That could be my niche in the market. I am the type of person people want in their home—clean, respectful, on time, clean up after myself, and do a quality job for a reasonable price."

Dan responded online: "I can help you with that. I'm Dan, engineer by trade, and I got let go from my job through a Reduction in Force. I'm happy to come take a look. I've been doing this all my life, and I won't take on the job if I can't do it."

When Dan gave his price estimate, the teacher was happy—so happy, in fact, that he hired Dan for three more jobs, and they had many long conversations. The teacher told him, "You should do this for a living. I can't tell you how many people in this neighborhood could use your services."

As co-chair of his Homeowners Association, the teacher spread the word. "Word of mouth is everything," says Dan. "I began thinking this might work."

In November 2016, Dan went onto Nextdoor and created a business page called Dan's Handyman Services. His biggest concern was he didn't yet have a sense of how far he'd have to go to get a market that could support his business. By December, he was getting calls on a daily basis, with 98 percent of them coming from Nextdoor.

"I was getting my name out, and as I completed my first jobs, I asked my customers to recommend me because you need four recommendations before your Nextdoor business page can go live. They were ecstatic to help me because they were happy with the work." Now he says, if he walks away from a job, and a customer has not complimented him, that's a sure sign he didn't do it well enough because 99.9 percent of the time people will tell you they like your work.

By mid-2017, Dan was fielding one to two calls per day and had been booked two to three weeks in advance since he announced his business online. His entire market has been within a 15-mile radius of Cordova and north Germantown (two suburbs of Memphis). "The area has a lot of demand because there are many homes 10 to 15 years old that are starting to need repairs and updates."

Dan's mantra became, "Yes, I can do that!" although he is careful to point out that he would never take on a job he is not qualified to do. He does not make what he did as an engineer, but there is another huge difference: he now loves what he does. He also has plans for how to expand his business and begin building his income.

Pam the Gym Owner

Pam fell in love with gymnastics in the eighth grade. She remembers the day she first saw her friends out on the playground doing handstands and backbends. She joined in, her small stature and gumby flexibility attracting the attention of the gymnastics coach. Pam was recruited to the school team and brought home a second place ribbon on beam just one month later.

After a truncated career as a competitive gymnast in college (University of Central Arkansas canceled their program while she was in attendance), she found a new passion for judging competitions—as well as a significant amount of income. After graduation, Pam moved to California, but she was drawn back to Arkansas when her little brother was diagnosed with cancer. She worked for a time in Little Rock and ran a gymnastics program for over 200 kids at a local YMCA.

After getting married in the early 1990s, Pam became a school teacher but found that she missed gymnastics terribly. Eventually, with the support of her husband, and without quitting her teaching job, Pam decided to open her own gym.

She created a business plan that would allow her to run a program during after-school hours. She found a small pole barn building in town that would only require an $8,000 investment to get started, and she set up shop.

"To start, I just tested local interest. I had a single tumbling strip, a balance beam, and a set of bars. I started really small and built up to 80 students within the first year." By 1994, Pam was teaching full-time and raising a two-year-old, plus running the gymnastics business. "It got to be too much, and by that time I knew the business would support me."

Pam finally quit her day job as a teacher and expanded her gymnastics offerings. Eventually the program she created grew to a lucrative 185 students ("which is big for a small town"), and outgrew her space.

Her next major business decision came in response to an offer from a construction company to construct a 6,000-square foot building and lease out a portion to her. She told him, "I can use the whole 6,000 feet myself!" So they sealed the deal: he built it and Pam bought the building outright by getting a bank loan to cover the full $130,000 cost of the space. Eventually

Pam's gym was almost fully paid off, with Pam as the sole owner.

After suffering through a divorce in 2007, the gym became Pam's sole source of income. "In 2008, at the height of the Great Recession, steel mills in town were laying off people left and right," says Pam ruefully. "I got down to 80 students and had to eliminate all non-essential employees. I had to go back to teaching some classes myself, and I recruited both my daughters to teach. I almost sacrificed my business during that time, but we made it."

In late 2016, Pam looked at her pole barn building and its metal walls that had always made it impossible to adequately heat the space in winter. She thought about the bare insulation that lured rodents to take up residence inside, seeking crumbs from the birthday parties she was forced to hold on the gym floor because she lacked a party room. She began planning an upgrade, one of the calculated risks that is part of running a business.

Then, in 2017, Pam got wind of a new gym opening in the next town 15 miles down the freeway, so she sped up the timeline for her upgrade. "At that time, I was down to a relatively small bank note, and I decided it was time to either invest or sellout. I obtained another mortgage, and put $70-80,000 back into the space."

Pam's gym now boasts a full-size gymnastics competition floor, all the Olympic gymnastic equipment, a foam pit, and a new kitchen and party space in a loft area built above the offices on the first floor. The space also allows her to showcase her athlete's trophies as well as doubling as bleacher seating for spectators when Pam hosts competitions.

"We also have new A/C and heating in the lobby and office spaces, and I had the contractor seal the cracks at the base of the building and install metal flashing to control the rodents.

"I waited to make these investments because I was too fearful and too cautious. It's a lot more space than I had dreamed it might be and the best money I ever spent. I only wish I had done it sooner."

Summary

As a mid-life career person seeking a way into the Independent Life, you will have competition. It will come from the droves of others like you who plan to make the leap within the next several years. A significant number of those competitors will be Millennials or younger, who are hungry and tech-savvy.

However, experience is a great teacher and valued in the marketplace. Your advantages as someone in mid-career include the self-knowledge and expertise you bring to your job, your passion, potentially greater savings, and flexibility later in life after your child-raising is done.

Perhaps the best advantage for you will be your day job. Research shows that the hybrid model of entrepreneurship, in which you start your own business while retaining your "day job," increases the chances of survival of your business by 30 percent compared to those who quit to launch a new business. Most likely this is because the "hybrid" phase will help you to determine if your business idea is really worth pursuing before you commit to doing so full time.

Knowing your advantages, if you are ready to make the leap, the most compelling question is, how do you start? Chapter 7 focuses on the early stages of self-employment, distilling the combined experience of ten Independent Lifers into principles for success and actionable advice.

CHAPTER 7

PRINCIPLES FOR SUCCESS IN SELF-EMPLOYMENT

"Give your best to every client, whether small or large. You never know to whom you are offering your gifts. If you did, you'd be humbled."

—Arupa Tesolin, Innovation author, speaker, trainer and founder of Velocified[89]

At age 25, after having won several international ballroom championship titles, Misha the Ballroom Studio Owner, who was born in Russia and grew up in the Ukraine, came to Memphis, Tennessee. He was done with his career as a professional competitive

[89] Tesolin, Arupa. "12 Power Thoughts for Creators Everywhere | LinkedIn." LinkedIn, April 17, 2014. https://www.linkedin.com/pulse/20140417164905-4785314-12-rules-for-a-heroes-destiny/.

dancer and was already hoping he would one day be able to open a dance business.

Initially, because he had signed a contract with a noncompete clause, he was considering a future with his own franchise working with the dance studio that hired him. "Actually, I can work very well for someone, I can follow orders and am very responsible by nature. The problem was my boss. I didn't respect him. It made work miserable, and he didn't leave me a choice."

Misha stuck it out for five years, learning the ropes of running a dance studio in America. During that time he saved as much of his salary as he could. "Saving is my most important advice," he says.

He built a financial cushion that allowed him to quit and open a studio an hour away in a much smaller market, but far enough to meet the distance specified by the non-compete clause in his contract. He then began his business career buoyed by the support of a few loyal students. His savings enabled him to wait out the three years required by his non-compete clause before returning to the much larger dance market in Memphis.

After three years, Misha returned and held the grand opening of his studio, which he christened Ultimate Ballroom. Over the course of five years, Ultimate has grown from a one-man operation to an award-winning studio with six dance instructors and hundreds of students, who are themselves passionate about dance. Several of his students are competing—and winning—in national pro-am competitions.

Getting the early stages right

Misha's story demonstrates many of the critical things to "do right" when you strike out on your own to become self-employed. According to both academic research[90] and the wisdom of our Independent Life case studies, these include:

1. Carefully think through the decision of whether and when to "quit your day job." Academic research on entrepreneurship in recent years has shown that hybrid entrepreneurship—starting a business while keeping your day job—is increasingly common, and there are good reasons for considering this model (see Chapter 6). In Misha's case, his day job served as training for eventually opening his own small business.

2. Save money. This will make your transition far easier, far less stressful, and could be one of the most important factors determining your success at the outset of self-employment. Savings can be used in lieu of borrowing money, if an initial investment is

---

[90] Raffiee, Joseph, and Jie Feng. "Should I Quit My Day Job?: A Hybrid Path to Entrepreneurship." *Academy of Management Journal* 57, no. 4 (August 1, 2014): 936–63. https://doi.org/10.5465/amj.2012.0522.

required to start your business. It can also get you through the lean start-up times while you are establishing yourself and building your clientele. Savings are also important as a long-term strategy for managing uneven income levels through time.

3. Take time to build your skills and, especially, to learn new skills that you are going to need in your business. Unless you are in communications already, this will include the basics of marketing plus a website or a business page on social media, and may include physical space or a product inventory.

4. Seek family support. This does not have to be financial, but research shows that the vast majority (80 to 90 percent) of small businesses in North America are family businesses.[91] If you have a spouse, you'll want to discuss it with him or her.

5. Maintain your network, try not to burn bridges, and possibly even begin scouting for your first customers. In 2017, almost half (45 percent) of self-employed reported that reaching out to potential clients was one of their key activities in preparing to go independent.

6. If one of your reasons for considering self-employment is the uncertainty of your current job, be

---

[91] Conway Center for Family Business. "Family Business Facts." Conway Center for Family Business, 2017.
http://www.familybusinesscenter.com/resources/family-business-facts/.

especially aware and sensitive to changes in your workplace. As Dan the Handyman says, you can tell when change is coming. It's far better to prepare for the worst, rather than hiding in your cubicle waiting for the next Reduction in Force!

More principles for success

Get your first customers

One of the most difficult obstacles to overcome when starting a new business is to find your first clients or customers. Because you are new, it takes a level of faith, familiarity, or favorable impressions on the part of clients to hire you. The key here is to cultivate your existing network of friends, potential customers, and potential collaborators (in the form of subcontractors, partners, or investors) to get your business off the ground. Be sure to include former, supportive employers in this mix, if possible.

If, like me, you begin pursuing self-employment partially because you are dissatisfied with your current position and you'd welcome a different job, the job application process might actually serve as a way to find your first clients as a contractor. While planning for an Independent Life, you can apply *in good faith* to positions that you want and would accept if offered.

Even if you are not offered the positions, if you make it through to the final candidate stage, this is a good chance to build or expand your network of people in your field. Your interviewers will feel like they know you somewhat as a result of the intensive interview process, and they might then be able to send clients your way knowing that you are currently self-employed part-time or considering self-employment.

This is exactly what happened to me. I applied for a job with the U.S. Fish and Wildlife Service, and though I didn't get it, I eventually got my second major client as a result of that interview process.

Although it goes without saying that giving your all to each client and customer is important, top performance for your very first clients and customers is critical. This is because word of mouth referrals and recommendations for new business are the primary way that people gain new clients.

Think about it. When you need to find a new doctor or hairdresser or someone to work on your computer or a good restaurant, what do you do? You ask your friends. You read reviews online.

So, when you get that first gig, jump on it, give it 150 percent, and don't worry if you spend extra time or money to get the job done. It will be well spent and come back to you many times over if your customers are happy and impressed.

Do not make the mistake I once did. When I began working with one new client on a trial basis, they asked me to take over a newsletter account and begin managing it. Difficulties in that process caused me to spend far more time than I normally would have to produce their first newsletter. When they saw that first invoice, even though I explained the issue, it must have been sticker shock because I never worked for them again. If I had eaten that cost and charged them what I knew the job would normally cost, they might still be my clients.

Set your rates, but don't sell yourself short

Be careful when setting your initial rates. In particular, take care not to set your initial rates too low. This is easy to do if you are inexperienced or hungry to be competitive.

I am also a firm believer in the maxim that you get what you pay for, and conversely, people tend to value that in which they have made an investment. You want your clients and customers to view hiring you or your business as a valued investment.

Research your competition, and use the many resources available online to help you calculate the rate you will need to charge to meet your new expenses and support yourself. Remember that it is difficult to increase rates once they have been set, but much easier to reduce them.

Some of the primary differences you need to include in your calculations:

- self-employment taxes (your social security, or FICA, and medicare taxes double because you assume the responsibility of paying for the employer's as well as the employee's share of these taxes)
- health insurance
- sick leave (time that you are unable to work and earn money because you are too ill)
- vacation time
- administrative time (business tasks that are not billable to any one client)
- overhead: office rental, out-of-pocket office expenses, insurance, or materials
- retirement

A clear understanding of these costs is important not only for setting appropriate rates, but also for giving you the ability to justify your costs to potential clients. Your justification should emphasize the value you provide, but you can also subtly point out that comparing your hourly rate to that of an employee is comparing apples to oranges. Many managers may not consider the fact that the cost of their employees usually ranges from 30 to 35 percent greater than their salary once benefits are included.

Also, when you are self-employed, you usually cannot claim unemployment insurance even if you lose all of your business.

<u>Build your clientele</u>

Many organizations will hire you for a small job as a means of trying out a new work relationship. If you perform well, these small jobs can lead to much larger projects. When I was initially hired by an agency to produce a 10-year retrospective report, I knew that they might be interested in hiring me on a longer-term contract. In essence, the project was an "interview" for a longer term position. Happy customers also become repeat customers, which can become the bread and butter of your business.

Use your network. Perhaps you are wondering if you really have a network. Your network includes anyone you have ever worked for or with and anyone you have ever interacted with in your chosen or a related field of interest, with one caveat. The interaction has to have been positive!

Use that network to let people know about your new business. Look for networking opportunities. Reams and reams have been written about how to network, which you can find online or in the recently released book, *Croissants vs. Bagels* by Robbie Samuels.

Use social media—I have found LinkedIn to be the most effective platform for my business, but that will vary for each individual. Build a website or a landing page. Offer to do work for a coveted client on a trial basis or offer your service to new customers at an introductory rate. Enter a contest, win, and use that win to market your business.

Burnish your reputation

Everyone I interviewed for this book confirms that referrals from existing clients is the primary way in which they get new business. It has been 100 percent of the new business I have received over the years. I once asked someone how they had found me, and they said, "Your reputation precedes you."

Dan the Handyman says, "Reputation is everything."

Ivan the Cinematographer says, "If you do a great job and go the extra mile, people will appreciate it."

Come up to speed

Perhaps you want to run your own business, but you feel as if work in your field—with its new technology and digital advances—has left you behind. Then consider investing in training.

If you plan to establish an internet-based business, I have some good news for you. As long as you have basic knowledge, skills, drive, and passion, the amazing thing is that even though you may be behind in terms of your awareness, expertise, and facility with some online tools, you can probably catch up! That's because (a) the rate of technological change is so fast, no one stays an expert for long without constant learning, and (b) there is a supply of on-demand services online to cover most areas in which you need expert assistance.

In fact, whenever I'm stumped or just need an easier way to accomplish a job, I go to g.o.d.—that's google on demand. I have found exactly the tool I need to accomplish tasks online countless times, simply by googling for it. If there is an app or a knowledge tool that you have a need for, chances are someone else has recognized the need and the service is provided online (for free or for a price, usually a fairly reasonable one). In fact, if you ever discover a need for a service that could be provided online but you cannot find it, that is a business opportunity!

The fluidity and ease of use of new business tools is the up side of today's online business environment and the multiplying number of cloud-based services. The downside is newbies entering the market can quickly be competitive with you as well, but that's okay because you will have passion for what you do. If you are always learning and always challenged and always interested in what you are doing, you'll have the edge.

<u>Prepare to learn new skills</u>

Every entrepreneur, especially those just starting out, becomes more of a jack-of-all-trades. That's because, unless you are extremely well-funded and can afford to hire all your extra talent, you will suddenly find yourself thrust into the world of finances as well as marketing, which also means the world wide web.

Today a huge portion of marketing occurs through the internet. In fact, the internet and the many tools that are constantly being developed and offered through the web are primary forces that have allowed so many new entrepreneurs to begin working for themselves.

The web has leveled the playing field of marketing and reaching potential customers. If you tend to say things like "I don't like computers," perhaps you need to reevaluate that relationship! Or perhaps you'll need to hire someone who *does* like them.

Another example of the need to expand your skill set is the accounting side of your business. If you are offering a service, you'll need to track your time, costs of materials and travel, and the tasks you have completed for your clients.

If you are making a product, you'll also have to track the cost of inputs and set an appropriate retail price, plus you will need to track your inventory and sales for tax purposes. You may also need more sophistication in the way that you track appointments or shipments of supplies.

Luckily, for all of these functions, there are now excellent services and apps available—you guessed it—online, and there may be other entrepreneurial souls out there who will be happy to assist you as well.

Your tax preparation will also change. You'll have to calculate self-employment taxes and more than likely set aside money for taxes to be paid quarterly. The way I manage that is by depositing my contract receipts into a business account, then paying myself a "salary" (minus the taxes that will be due) into a personal bank account and using the part I withheld to pay quarterly estimated taxes.

If you hire contractors from time to time, you'll have to send them 1099s. If you start a retail business or hire employees, your taxes will become even more complicated, and you will probably need to work with an accountant. However, even with an accountant you'll need to learn what is required and put in place procedures for tracking your costs, wages, benefits, profit, etc.

Beyond these basics, you will only remain competitive in what you are doing by constantly learning, adding to your skill set, gaining experience, and improving your results. Ivan the Cinematographer explains how this works in his business, but this scenario holds true for everyone who is self-employed.

"You can be hired for a large company to direct and produce films only for that company. But people who do this pretty much do one thing everyday. They get out of date very quickly and lose their skills. They lock themselves into that one thing. Whereas people in my field view freelance professional as synonymous with quality. They want someone who has been exposed to many projects, not the same thing all the time. Variety in jobs is important."

<u>Keep excellent records</u>

Keep detailed records, as needed, to track your work, your costs, your income, and your taxes. For example, as Dan the Handyman began his service, the only way he could determine whether he was bidding his jobs at a rate that was fair (both to his clients and to himself) was by keeping detailed records of each job, including the cost of materials and the amount of his time required to complete each one.

The records allowed him to send accurate invoices to his clients, but more importantly, it made his bidding of new jobs increasingly accurate. He was able to distinguish the jobs that made him money versus those that put him into the red.

Sophie the Wildlife Artist emphasizes the importance of keeping track of expenses and sales if you are in a selling market. She tracks all her invoices in a spreadsheet, and she puts a checkmark by everything that requires payment of sales taxes. When she sells prints or other products in California, she has to pay state sales tax. Sometimes her sales are combined with contract work as well, so good record-keeping is essential.

Over the years, I have found that when I invoice my clients showing detailed records for the activities I have conducted each day, it tends to impress them or at the very least make them comfortable that they are getting their money's worth. Otherwise, "communications" can sound mighty vague. Keeping such records, particularly for multiple clients each day, requires developing the habit.

Specialization often works

Becoming self-employed, particularly if you are working alone, will usually require a degree of specialization. In my case, I combined a detailed knowledge of the hows, whys, and whos of conservation with communications skills and online communications tools (which I had to learn from scratch).

A niche, or highly specialized, business is good because it will allow you to work around the huge companies or the crowded field of mainstream competitors who may not fully meet the needs of your niche clientele. On the other hand, sometimes the market is well-defined, but there are places where no one is meeting that need.

However, while specialization is good for business, try not to put all your eggs in one basket by relying too much on one client or one source of customers. When I first began working for myself full-time, I had one client, then two. Eventually I focused all of my time on one of those clients (for a variety of reasons), and after about three years that client was hit by a funding cut.

During lean times, contract workers hired to augment the work of an organization's staff are usually the first to go because the organization wants to protect its full-timers. After that, I understood the value of multiple clients and diversification!

Accept reality

Few business ventures go exactly as planned. In my experience, few individual contracts go exactly as planned either.

As humans, we are constantly imagining scenarios and making up stories in our minds for what we envision, what we want, and how we think things should be. This holds true for our businesses, especially, into which we put a large part of our time, energy, dreams, and ego. This can make it hard when the story takes a turn that we did not expect, or worse yet, that we do not want.

The turn for the worse may not threaten your income or business success at all, but instead threaten your pride or your sense of what you can do and are capable of. This has happened to me at various times while working on long-term contracts. In working with one client team, I offered, on the basis of my past job experience, to start conducting "cold call" outreach to potential new conservation partners, and was met with silence—the polite way of saying no in the 21st century.

Pam the Gym Owner recommends handling difficult realities this way. "Develop protocols in your business as you grow, the clients will teach you! They will push you into areas where you don't want to be. To avoid finding yourself there again, you'll develop standards and norms for how your business is run. It has taken me years to develop and refine mine."

Another potential source of disappointment, of course, is failure—and by this I mean failure with a little f (not loss of your business). This could be when a client works with you but does not extend the relationship at the end of your contract, opting instead to work with someone else. This could include when you attract the interests of a new customer, who ultimately decides your company is not for them.

When that happens, the best you can do is try to maintain a cordial relationship, even if it is just to say good-by, and learn from the experience. Conduct your own post-mortem on what went wrong and how you could improve next time, even ask for feedback from the client or customer you lost. In the end, not everyone will be the right fit for you and vice versa.

Try not to obsess over your fears and failures, which is much easier said than done. As Mitch Matthews, author of *Dream Job: Redefined* said in a recent podcast interview[92], "Worry is simply unproductive imagination." His recommendation for dealing with valid issues that worry us is not to deny the worry but to replace it, consciously, with different thoughts or— even better—some positive action, no matter how small, that can address the source of worry.

Failure with a big F, the demise of your business, is always possible, but if you begin sensing that big F on the horizon, there are many ways to modify what you are doing before accepting defeat. For example, on the basis of much thoughtful feedback, Maurrean the App Developer pivoted from her original market focus on in-home techs to students preparing to graduate with a trade skill, certificate, or associate's degree.

---

[92] Chandler Bolt. How to Punch Worry in the Face with Mitch Matthews. Self-Publishing School Podcast. Accessed April 18, 2018. https://self-publishingschool.com/sps-020-punch-worry-face-mitch-matthews/

Your setbacks will be unique to you, but you can rest assured they will occur. Be prepared for that. Maintain flexibility and openness to the facts of each situation, which can mean letting go of your own internal dramas about what is happening. Each setback must be dealt with on a case-by-case basis.

"A winner is just a loser who tried one more time."[93] Those words from George M. Moore Jr. are about more than inspiration, they are about reality!

Pam the Gym Owner has this advice: "Financially, times may get tough, and you'll need others to believe in you. You'll need family or friends that allow you to go out and fail, learn, and improve. You'll need people who will support you while you're building your business."

The important thing is not to give up, not to let the disappointment drag you down, and to refocus on doing your very best. In your moments of greatest disappointment, when you really feel the pressure, amidst your worst mistakes—that is when you have to tell yourself, "tomorrow is another day." Then take the day off because, as your own boss, you can!

---

[93] Moore, George. 2018. "A Quote by George Moore." Goodreads.Com. 2018. https://www.goodreads.com/quotes/897172-a-winner-is-just-a-loser-who-tried-one-more.

<u>Make choices for the life you want.</u>

In one way or another, all the Independent Lifers featured in this book are telling us that an important aspect of self-employment or running your own business is to balance work and life. Yes, you will be inspired and tempted and even required to work long hours at times. Do not lose track, amidst the exhilaration and hustle, of what is truly important: your kids, your spouse, your friendships, exercise, and time to relax and experience the world.

Ivan the Cinematographer had this epiphany very explicitly as he was avidly pursuing his fledgling career in Hollywood. During a series of lunches with famous and highly successful people (astutely set up as part of his master's thesis), Ivan began to realize that most of the people he interviewed came across as sad, along with being very wealthy.

"The personal aspect of their life had been left behind," Ivan explains. "It made me realize, 'I want to be this guy, but I want to have a life too.' I realized I'm working really hard toward something that may not make me happy. I knew then that I could not focus only on my career, and I'm glad I had this realization early. It made me slow down my career." It also led him back to Brazil, his native country, where he eventually met his wife!

You may also need to make tough choices from time to time. About a year into working for my second major client, a government agency offered me a four-year term position. That meant I would become an employee for four years, but at the end of that time there'd be no guarantee of being hired permanently. The position would also prohibit me from working for anyone else outside of my regular work hours.

The offer was tempting because the pay was good, I really enjoyed the people I was working with, and I supported the agency's mission. However, I began to think about what would happen after four years: without the ability to continue contract work, I would have to start again from scratch. I said no.

It was a good decision because four years later marked a significant downturn in funding for that agency's program. I feel certain my position would have been cut entirely. Instead, during those four years I had built up a body of work and a few more clients. More importantly, all the people both in and outside the agency with whom I'd been working for the past four years knew my work *as a contractor* rather than as an employee.

This helped to build that priceless "word of mouth." I'm not sure the extent to which this would have been the case if I were a term employee. The narrative might have looked more like, "They hired her, then after four years they let her go." Not good!

Know when to say no

Inevitably, in running your own business you will have to say no: to potential clients, to work that you do not have time for, to vendors who want your business, to contractors or employees. Don't be afraid to say no, but choose your no's carefully, and deliver them gently.

After I'd been in business for about five or six years, I was offered a job by a state agency that looked, initially, straight forward. However, as I looked more closely I found that it would entail editing a 100-page document using a spreadsheet of more than 500 comments for various pages (rather than the use of a sleek and effective online co-editing tool such as google docs).

I decided to do a random check of the comments and discovered that I would not be able to handle the vast majority of them as an editor. Instead I would have to track down several people within the agency to obtain key decisions.

I knew that hunting down busy people was a thankless task and the time required to do so could easily mushroom. Moreover, the budget for the project was tight. I then had a good reason (insufficient available time) to turn down the job. In addition, I was able to offer the agency some insight when I turned them down (an estimate of how long it could take and the need for further internal review).

Get your family's support

Starting a business is difficult, time-intensive, and involves significant amounts of both risk and personal investment. It is important to have the support or at least consent of key family members.

A 2017 survey of highly successful business owners found that 42 percent have a family member involved in their business in some capacity, and business owners have used their own or family savings to finance their business. The involvement of family members can provide a competitive advantage, since family members will be more invested in the enterprise, both literally and figuratively.[94]

Be nice

Ivan the Cinematographer says it best: "For you to be a successful cinematographer you have to be nice, fast, and good—in that order. From my point of view, the ability to work with someone is part of your marketing. Just be nice!"

---

[94] Bank of America. "U.S. Trust Study Finds Entrepreneurs Choose Career Path of Most Resistance | Bank of America Newsroom," May 23, 2016. http://newsroom.bankofamerica.com/press-releases/global-wealth-and-investment-management/us-trust-study-finds-entrepreneurs-choose-car.

This advice applies across the business world, not just cinematography. Research has shown that likability is responsible for positive outcomes in life. In his recently published book *"Popular: The Power of Likability in a Status-Obsessed World,"* Dr. Mitch Prinstein, a clinical psychologist at the University of North Carolina at Chapel Hill, says, "Being liked creates opportunities for learning and for new kinds of life experiences that help somebody gain an advantage."[95]

Top reasons small businesses fail

Maybe you've heard the statistic that half of new businesses fail in the first year. In fact, the Small Business Administration says this is not the case, it's more like 30 percent within the first two years, and it is not until year five that the percentage rises to 50. However, *avoid* these common mistakes to help your new business to succeed:

- Lack of understanding of your market. Find an underserved or unmet need in your market (a niche) and then fill it rather than competing against many established businesses.

- Lack of a business plan. Although many of our Independent Lifers skipped this stage, there is a reason why the business plan was

---

[95] Nir, Sarah Maslin. "Be Nice — You Won't Finish Last." *The New York Times*, April 7, 2017, sec. Education Life. https://www.nytimes.com/2017/04/07/education/edlife/be-nice-you-wont-finish-last.html.

invented. It helps you to scope your market and, by calculating costs and outputs, will help you pencil out whether your business can make enough money to support you.

- Insufficient financing. It's important to be realistic and best when you can use your own savings, without borrowing or with limited loans, to get your business up and running.

- Bad location or internet marketing. People shop online more every year. It's essential to create a good website and social media presence online.

- Unwillingness to adapt. The business environment is constantly changing and people's needs for your business will change along with it. Don't be afraid to "pivot," make adjustments, learn, or add to your business offerings.

- Expanding too fast. This can result in the inability to find business to cover the costs of your expansion, or it can mean creating new demand that you are unable to fulfill. When considering expansion, it's best to "treat the expansion like you're starting all over again."[96]

---

[96] Investopedia Staff. "Top 6 Reasons New Businesses Fail." Investopedia, October 29, 2010. https://www.investopedia.com/slideshow/top-6-reasons-new-businesses-fail/.

Summary

Starting your own business can be both exhilarating and grueling. The universe of tasks that you will need to accomplish will expand by a factor of three or four compared to that of your role as employee. You'll be learning constantly.

By paying careful attention to key principles for how to start a business and by listening to the advice of Independent Lifers contained in these pages, you will increase your chances of success significantly.

The next question to address is what your business might be. That depends on you and your unique talents, interests, and skills. However, it never hurts to get a sense of the landscape of opportunities that exist in the world of work. Chapter 8 provides reconnaissance that highlights where the near-term opportunities are likely to be found.

CHAPTER 8

WHERE THE OPPORTUNITIES ARE

"Of the IT and Business executives we surveyed, 85 percent indicate they plan to increase their organization's use of independent freelance workers over the next year."

—Accenture, a business strategy and tech consulting firm working with more than three-quarters of the Fortune Global 500[97]

Having toured the world of work in America since the mid-20th century, we have found it changed radically. Although great jobs still exist, the value and security

---

[97] Accenture. "Technology Vision 2017." Accenture LLP. Accessed March 18, 2018. https://www.accenture.com/t20170321T032507__w__/us-en/_acnmedia/Accenture/next-gen-4/tech-vision-2017/pdf/Accenture-TV17-Full.pdf.

of traditional jobs has declined for four decades. Side hustles through the so-called "sharing economy," while valuable, are unlikely to be your savior, and the Fourth Industrial Revolution is poised to cause unemployment, dislocation, and upheaval on a scale the world may never have seen before.

Part I of this book laid out these mega-trends that are pushing many people the world over to consider self-employment. Aside from the push factors, the positives pulling people toward their own businesses include the intrinsic rewards of creating a life in which your security and fulfillment is based on your own initiative and capabilities rather than your company's stock price on Wall Street.

Part II of this book provided an overview of the qualities that all successful entrepreneurs have in common: passion, a great work ethic, people skills, and a touch of courage. It also provided some time-tested principles for success, as well as a closer look at how people are making mid-career switches to self-employment.

How you implement those principles in your own foray into freelancing or entrepreneurship will depend on the type of business that you choose. You may be asking yourself, what next?

What kind of business will you pursue? Will it be in your current career field, will it be something related, or will it be scaling up a side hustle into full-time, independent? Perhaps it will be something completely new that matches your always-developing talents and skills? In a world that is rapidly changing, where even the experts admit that we can't imagine what many jobs in the future will be, it's a good idea to get a sense of the possibilities.

A business opportunity is where your interests and skills overlap with the needs of someone else. What follows in this chapter is a listing of job skills, business sectors, and future needs on the horizon that business and government think tanks have identified as likely to be most in demand in the coming decades.

Recent reports focusing on the future of work concentrate on the type of jobs, both existing and emerging, that will become available. However, these trends can also be viewed as opportunities for *self-employment*. Where there is demand, there will be business opportunities.

Technology will create more jobs (and more business opportunities)

How technology will affect the future of work is not all bad news! Technology tends to create more jobs than it destroys over time and could ultimately "more than offset jobs lost to automation."[98] Whether this happens depends on job creation and retraining by businesses and governments for the purpose of managing short-term labor displacement.

Worldwide, one billion more people are expected to enter the consuming class by 2025, which means that global consumption will also grow, primarily in emerging economies. But demand from these new consumers will ripple out to the economies that export to those countries. The McKinsey Global Institute, the world's leading private sector think tank, estimates that 300 million to 365 million new jobs could be created worldwide from the impact of rising incomes.[99]

The trick is navigating this period of change and making it through, not only whole, but in better shape than you began.

If you are someone who is cognizant of the trends going on around you; if you are interested or, even better, enthusiastic about learning new skills; if you can be a keen observer of the problems that people

---

[98] Manyika, James, Susan Lund, Michael Chui, Jacques Bughin, Jonathan Woetzel, Parul Batra, Ryan Ko, and Saurabh Sanghvi. "Jobs Lost, Jobs Gained," December 2017. https://www.mckinsey.com/global-themes/future-of-organizations-and-work/what-the-future-of-work-will-mean-for-jobs-skills-and-wages.

[99] Manyika, James, Susan Lund, Michael Chui, Jacques Bughin, Jonathan Woetzel, Parul Batra, Ryan Ko, and Saurabh Sanghvi. "Jobs Lost, Jobs Gained," December 2017. https://www.mckinsey.com/global-themes/future-of-organizations-and-work/what-the-future-of-work-will-mean-for-jobs-skills-and-wages

are experiencing and figure out a way to solve them—then there will be a demand for what you have to offer.

Increasingly, in the coming decades, it will be possible to meet that demand as a free agent, rather than as the employee of a company. Large companies across a wide spectrum of industries are, themselves, anticipating this change in their work forces.

"In five years or less, the presumptive judgments around full-time employment and freelancers will flip completely. Compared to traditional full-time employment, talent marketplaces will provide workers with improved earning opportunities, more rewarding work, secure benefits, and respected credentials."[100]

New and emerging job categories

The Future of Jobs report[101] produced by the World Economic Forum in 2016 (based on a worldwide survey of human resource officers and executives) anticipates the following new and emerging job categories to become critically important by the year 2020.

---

[100] Accenture. "Technology Vision 2017." Accenture LLP. Accessed March 18, 2018.
https://www.accenture.com/t20170321T032507__w__/us-en/_acnmedia/Accenture/next-gen-4/tech-vision-2017/pdf/Accenture-TV17-Full.pdf.
[101] World Economic Forum. "The Future of Jobs." World Economic Forum, January 2016.
http://www3.weforum.org/docs/WEF_Future_of_Jobs.pdf.

Data analysts will be needed to take on "big data," the term used to describe the burgeoning streams of information being captured from a variety of sources, including new technologies.

Specialized sales representatives will be needed in almost every industry to explain their technological innovations and new offerings to business, government, or consumer audiences.

Self-employment/jobs in continued demand

The top categories of self-employment as of 2017 are

- Construction and trades (19.6%,)
- Retail (10.9%)
- Real estate (10.7%)
- Consulting (10.3%)

Even careers more traditionally associated with large institutions are represented, such as health and wellness, at 2.6 percent.[102]

Certain fields are already difficult to recruit for and will likely experience a growth in demand for qualified people over the period 2015-2020. These include

---

[102] Upwork, Freelancers Union. "Freelancing in America: 2017 Survey - Upwork." Upwork, October 27, 2017.
https://www.upwork.com/i/freelancing-in-america/2017/.

computers and information technology, mathematical applications, architecture, and engineering.

Overall spending on technology could increase by more than 50 percent between 2015 and 2030. About half will be spent on information technology services, both in-house IT workers within companies and external or outsourced tech consulting jobs.[103]

McKinsey Global Institute reports[104] the job categories with the highest percentage growth (after automation) will include:

- health-care providers
- professionals such as engineers, scientists, accountants, and analysts
- IT professionals and other technology specialists
- managers and executives, whose work cannot easily be replaced by machines
- educators, especially in emerging economies with young populations
- creatives, a small but growing category of artists, entertainers, and designers

---

[103] Manyika, James, Susan Lund, Michael Chui, Jacques Bughin, Jonathan Woetzel, Parul Batra, Ryan Ko, and Saurabh Sanghvi. "Jobs Lost, Jobs Gained," December 2017. https://www.mckinsey.com/global-themes/future-of-organizations-and-work/what-the-future-of-work-will-mean-for-jobs-skills-and-wages.

[104] Manyika, James, Susan Lund, Michael Chui, Jacques Bughin, Jonathan Woetzel, Parul Batra, Ryan Ko, and Saurabh Sanghvi. "Jobs Lost, Jobs Gained," December 2017. https://www.mckinsey.com/global-themes/future-of-organizations-and-work/what-the-future-of-work-will-mean-for-jobs-skills-and-wages.

- building and related professions, including painters, construction, and maintenance
- manual and service jobs in unpredictable environments such as people's homes or the outdoors: personal care aids, landscapers, groundskeepers

The special case of health care

Worldwide, by 2030 the number of people aged 65 or older is likely to have increased by 300 million people compared to 2014.[105] In America, the 65-and-over age group is expected to double by 2060 compared to 2016, making this group nearly one-quarter of the population.[106]

These statistics alone are enough to illustrate how the demand for health care is going to rise over the coming decades. Furthermore, the U.S. Bureau of Labor Statistics predicts that demand for personal care aides will increase by 72 percent from 2012 to 2022.[107]

---

[105] Manyika, James, Susan Lund, Michael Chui, Jacques Bughin, Jonathan Woetzel, Parul Batra, Ryan Ko, and Saurabh Sanghvi. "Jobs Lost, Jobs Gained," December 2017. https://www.mckinsey.com/global-themes/future-of-organizations-and-work/what-the-future-of-work-will-mean-for-jobs-skills-and-wages.

[106] Mather, Mark. "Fact Sheet: Aging in the United States – Population Reference Bureau." Population Reference Bureau, January 13, 2016. https://www.prb.org/aging-unitedstates-fact-sheet/.

[107] Vilorio, Dennis. "Self-Employment: What to Know to Be Your Own Boss : Career Outlook: U.S. Bureau of Labor Statistics." United States Bureau of Labor Statistics. Accessed March 28, 2018. https://www.bls.gov/careeroutlook/2014/article/self-employment-what-to-know-to-be-your-own-boss.htm.

In my own personal life, with a father who is suffering from Alzheimer's, I have seen how there is a lack of games, activities, and gadgets that can be used by people with declining powers of cognition. The problem is, the decline is slow. Where are the materials and games—preferably in physical form—that can make navigating this decline less harrowing and boring? In addition to a focus on prevention and treatment, we need a kind of entertainment or education industry for the elderly who are experiencing a kind of childhood in reverse, but which is also respectful to the competent adults they once were.

Human Resources

As more of us peel off into the Independent Life, we will ourselves create the need for better ways to match skills and people with companies and others who need our skills. According to one expert, this means human resource specialists will have to completely rethink everything "from how you write the ad, the job description, speed of hire, [the] recruitment system, employee assessments, rapid on boarding, and having adequate performance based learning support to attract . . . talent."[108]

Ironically, even with jobageddon looming, in the short-term companies are facing accelerating retire-

---

[108] Tesolin, Arupa. "Work Is Broken - This Is Jobageddon | LinkedIn," August 1, 2014. https://www.linkedin.com/pulse/20140801141146-4785314-job-sharknado-looming/.

ments in the U.S. and Canada (perhaps many of those retirees are headed toward a second Independent Life career). This means that even with zero job growth, companies will be "scrambling to get that next hire in the door, train them, keep them happy and retain them—and, just as importantly, keep clients and customers happy."[109] All of this translates into a demand for training services.

The changing nature of work and in-demand skills

As the rate of job change accelerates, it makes more sense to focus on the skills and attributes that will become more valued with time.

<u>Social skills—people persons rejoice!</u>

"Soft" skills such as persuasion, emotional intelligence, and coaching others will become increasingly important as AI and automation take over many of the more narrow technical tasks, such as programming or equipment operation. Why? Because it's easy to program a robot to provide answers by identifying patterns or anomalies in a vast stream of data, but it's difficult to program one to ask the right question. "In essence, technical skills will need to be sup-

---

[109] Tesolin, Arupa. "Work Is Broken - This Is Jobageddon | LinkedIn," August 1, 2014. https://www.linkedin.com/pulse/20140801141146-4785314-job-sharknado-looming/.

plemented with strong social and collaboration skills."[110]

In fact, some of the most durable human roles in the digitalized economy will be those that are the most inherently social. These include for example, executives and managers of people and work in which interaction with people is an expected part of the package: massage, personal care and grooming, sports, many fields of medicine, and counseling.

<u>Retraining for second and third starts</u>

The accelerating nature of technological and job change means that the need for people and small businesses who can facilitate retraining, reorganizing, and partnerships between businesses and educational institutions is likely to explode, particularly if government-led retraining initiatives do not materialize.

The Future of Jobs report notes, "Across nearly all industries, the impact of technological and other changes is shortening the shelf-life of employees' existing skill sets."[111]

---

[110] World Economic Forum. "The Future of Jobs." World Economic Forum, January 2016.
http://www3.weforum.org/docs/WEF_Future_of_Jobs.pdf.
[111] World Economic Forum. "The Future of Jobs." World Economic Forum, January 2016.
http://www3.weforum.org/docs/WEF_Future_of_Jobs.pdf.

The same pressures that cause older employees to fear job loss or consider the Independent Life, are in themselves an opportunity. There is also a pressing need to find ways of using the accumulated experience of older employees to avoid loss of irreplaceable knowledge and skills.[112]

Flexible working arrangements

As more people work for themselves, both Independent Lifers and businesses will increasingly connect and collaborate remotely. Internet businesses are increasing exponentially, and a large chunk of them offer services that allow people to leverage the internet for work (think webinars and web meetings), data capture, analysis and storage (think Survey Monkey and google drive), and project management (think Trello and Monday)—all while saving on the costs of travel.

Co-meeting spaces such as WeWork or ShareDesk and sites that bring job searchers and/or freelancers together (think Muse, Wealthy Affiliate, or Virtual-Vocations) are also becoming highly popular.

---

[112] Manyika, James, Susan Lund, Michael Chui, Jacques Bughin, Jonathan Woetzel, Parul Batra, Ryan Ko, and Saurabh Sanghvi. "Jobs Lost, Jobs Gained," December 2017. https://www.mckinsey.com/global-themes/future-of-organizations-and-work/what-the-future-of-work-will-mean-for-jobs-skills-and-wages.

Emerging business sectors

As technologies advance and job requirements change, it's not just on-the-job skills requirements that are changing. New industries are being born or coming to prominence in the 21st century. The following is a list of relatively new business sectors with both high growth and a high ability to create positive change in the world. This list is based on my own knowledge background, so it is most assuredly not a comprehensive list.

The restoration economy is taking off

The restoration economy includes ecological restoration, environmental mitigation, pollution control, and cleanup. Restoration can mean everything from planting trees to regrading for natural topography to long-term wildlife monitoring to the re-creation of entire ecosystems such as grasslands or wetlands.

Complex restoration projects require input from many different specialties, including landscape planning and design, environmental sciences, data collection and monitoring, finance, and negotiation. Restoration employs experts in everything from GIS and remote sensing to machine operation of highly specialized equipment. The hands-on portion of restoration could be thought of as "maintenance and construction in the great outdoors."

Restoration jobs fit the profile of those that will not be easily automated, as they involve working in an inherently unpredictable environment—the great outdoors. In addition, all conservation is local, so many of these jobs are unlikely to be exported.

Research shows that restoration jobs are roughly half white-collar planners, designers, and engineers and about half "green-collar"—those doing actual earth moving, site construction, and field monitoring.

"Because restoration work is labor-intensive, the money goes to people instead of machines, and every $1 million invested generates 33 jobs on average," compared to 5.2 jobs per $1 million invested in the oil industry.[113]

An acceleration of learning accelerators

This new industry arises out of the need to train workers in new skills in a way that does not require another college degree. As noted in Chapter 3, an education to at least the associate degree level is likely to become more important in advanced economies, while starting life with an enormous debt burden from college can make it difficult to save—almost a prerequisite for launching into the Independent Life.

---

[113] Zwick, Steve. "Ten Things You Need To Know About The Restoration Economy." Ecosystem Marketplace (blog). Accessed March 18, 2018. https://www.forest-trends.org/ecosystem_marketplace/ten-things-need-know-restoration-economy/.

Tech "boot camps" and code schools, such as the General Assembly, focus on producing skilled people for the IT pipeline, although they are still relatively expensive. However, in the near-future, additional and completely new training functions will likely be met this way.[114]

Demand for digital literacy is strong

Marketing and communications people, take heed. The need for far more people in the workplace to attain digital literacy may need to be addressed through broad awareness campaigns. Past campaigns, such as those targeted at changing unhealthy behaviors—smoking and a lifestyle leading to obesity—have been particularly successful.

Digital literacy campaigns need to target youth and underrepresented groups with tailored, vivid messages that show them how computer and software skills can be the key, not just to jobs but careers of their *own* making.[115]

---

[114] Muro, Mark, Sifan Liu, Jacob Whiton, and Siddharth Kulkarni. "Digitalization and the American Workforce." The Brookings Institution, November 2017. https://www.brookings.edu/research/digitalization-and-the-american-workforce/.
[115] Muro, Mark, Sifan Liu, Jacob Whiton, and Siddharth Kulkarni. "Digitalization and the American Workforce." The Brookings Institution, November 2017. https://www.brookings.edu/research/digitalization-and-the-american-workforce/.

Changing the world for the better, one business at a time

Social business programs, pioneered by Nobel Peace Prize winner Muhammad Yunus, have caught on around the world. Yunus defines social business as "a non-dividend company dedicated to solving human problems."[116] (In my view, you can include in that the problems we have created for ourselves by degrading ecosystems.)

Social entrepreneurs design businesses expressly so that they can make a difference in the world by making money. This may be a structure as simple as donating a product, along with each consumer purchase, to those in need. It may be far more revolutionary, completely redesigning a supply chain and production process to become more ethical, transparent, and sustainable.[117]

Some U.S. universities and others around the world are building social business programs, including Yunus Social Business Centers (YSBCs). There are social business design competitions and social busi-

---

[116] Yunus, Muhammad. A World of Three Zeroes. Melbourne | London: Scribe Publications, 2017.
[117] Monocle. "The Social Impact Entrepreneurs Making A Difference - UNLIMITED by UBS," November 9, 2016.
https://www.unlimited.world/monocle/when-does-making-a-difference-mean-more-than-money.

ness academia conferences held each year in November.[118]

However, running a successful social business does not require a business degree. The MakeSense online platform is available to anyone. The MakeSense community provides immediate access to a worldwide network of consultants, all eager to help new social businesses succeed by offering ideas and support for entrepreneurs in countries around the world.

In his book, *A World of Three Zeroes* (zero poverty, zero unemployment, zero carbon), Yunus explains the variety of opportunities that are ripe for social business development. Most technology for social purposes, he says, has to be adapted from technologies that were originally aimed at the wealthiest sectors of society, to maximize profits.

Rather than designing for the 1 percent to maximize profit, he maintains we need to design for the bottom where the social and economic problems are. He describes the need for technologies that are not only cheaper, "but also simpler, upgradable, exchangeable for the next model, extremely durable, and more efficient in addressing poor people's needs."[119]

---

[118] Yunus, Muhammad. *A World of Three Zeroes*. Melbourne | London: Scribe Publications, 2017.
[119] Yunus, Muhammad. *A World of Three Zeroes*. Melbourne | London: Scribe Publications, 2017.

Yunus also identifies the need for a set of specially designed financial institutions that can provide the world's unbanked with all kinds of financial services designed exclusively for them.

"Given the power of human creativity, especially as enhanced by today's amazing breakthroughs in technology, any destination is reachable. But while trillions of dollars are invested in developing robotics and artificial intelligence for military and commercial purposes, there is little interest in applying technology to overcome the massive human problems of the world."[120]

Outdoor recreation: one of the largest business sectors in America

There is a vast and growing literature concerning the benefits, both direct and indirect, that people derive from nature, in the form of healthy, natural habitats and landscapes. The importance of the outdoor recreation sector has long been recognized by the industry, but has recently gained national recognition.

In 2016, in a unanimous vote of both the House of Representatives and the U.S. Senate, Congress endorsed the proposal to add the economic impact of

---

[120] Yunus, Muhammad. *A World of Three Zeroes*. Melbourne | London: Scribe Publications, 2017.

the outdoor recreation industry to the annual calculation of gross domestic product (GDP).[121]

In 2018, the Bureau of Economic Analysis released its first prototype statistics, estimating that outdoor recreation accounted for 2.0 percent of the U.S. economy ($373.7 billion in 2016). The outdoor recreation economy grew 3.8 percent in 2016, compared with the overall U.S. economy's 2.8 percent growth that year.[122]

Estimates by the Outdoor Industry Association show that from 2012 to 2017, outdoor recreation consumer spending increased by 27 percent in the U.S. They place outdoor recreation consumer spending just behind the healthcare and financial services industries, and far ahead of pharmaceuticals, motor vehicles, fuels, and education.[123]

To the extent that well-managed advances in automation can be used to create a shorter work week, Americans are increasingly likely to spend that time outdoors. According to the OIA (2017), the United States is globally recognized as the leader in outdoor

---

[121] Blevins, Jason. "Outdoor Industry Will Be Added to the Calculus of the Nation's Gross Domestic Product." The Denver Post, November 29, 2016. https://www.denverpost.com/2016/11/29/outdoor-industry-gross-domestic-product/.

[122] US Department of Commerce, B. E. A. "Bureau of Economic Analysis." Bureau of Economic Analysis, February 14, 2018.
https://www.bea.gov/newsreleases/industry/orsa/orsanewsrelease.htm.

[123] Outdoor Industry Association. "The Outdoor Recreation Economy." Outdoor Industry Association, 2017.
https://outdoorindustry.org/advocacy/.

recreation. The outdoor economy includes guiding and services in the inherently unpredictable (and often breathtakingly beautiful) outdoors. It also includes food, lodging, park service, and education.[124]

However, career opportunities also exist for those who produce the constantly improving array of specialized gear required for climbing, kayaking, board sailing, skiing, camping, horseback riding, hunting, fishing, and the list goes on. The outdoor recreation industry needs product developers, small and large retailers, and many other professionals.

Artificial intelligence

The very force that is poised to cause massive disruption to both industries and workers represents an opportunity to those with the programming skills to take advantage of it. Increasingly, to remain competitive, companies will need to expand their AI capabilities in the realms of customer service as well as internal operations.

There will be a need for experts to help design their AI capabilities and incorporate such systems into their user interface (UX/UI) teams. This will be another arena ripe for employee training as well as

---

[124] Outdoor Industry Association. "The Outdoor Recreation Economy." Outdoor Industry Association, 2017. https://outdoorindustry.org/advocacy/.

freelancers who can take advantage of existing AI toolkits.[125]

Roger Dickey, the CEO of Gigster (a web design and software development sharing platform) has identified complex knowledge work services like software development, design, legal, and financial work as the next frontier for the "gig economy."[126] If these are opportunities for work sharing platforms, they are also opportunities for independent freelancers!

Creatives

Creatives include entertainers, artists, and designers. Three factors will contribute to a growing demand for creatives:

- AI and automation may continue the trend toward shorter work hours around the globe.
- Rising incomes in emerging economies will create more disposable wealth and greater demand for entertainment.
- Creativity is a "soft" skill that can be difficult to program, moreover, people are likely to con-

---

[125] Accenture"Technology Vision 2017." Accenture LLP. Accessed March 18, 2018. https://www.accenture.com/t20170321T032507__w__/us-en/_acnmedia/Accenture/next-gen-4/tech-vision-2017/pdf/Accenture-TV17-Full.pdf.
[126] Accenture "Technology Vision 2017." Accenture LLP. Accessed March 18, 2018. https://www.accenture.com/t20170321T032507__w__/us-en/_acnmedia/Accenture/next-gen-4/tech-vision-2017/pdf/Accenture-TV17-Full.pdf.

tinue seeking out art and entertainment produced by other people.

Who are likely to be the losers?

According to McKinsey Global Institute, the activities
most susceptible to automation will be physical ones
in predictable environments (machine operators, food
prep workers) and collection/processing of data (par-
alegals, accountants). However, while automation
may hit such jobs the hardest, employment may not
decline. Rather, these occupations may change significantly.[127]

In addition, we've seen that those with a lower level
of education are already losing out on "good jobs,"
while education to at least the associate level is going to be increasingly important for job or entrepreneurial success in the U.S. and other advanced
economies.

Summary

Jobageddon could turn into a flowering of personal
potential for those able to take advantage of its
trends.

---

[127] Manyika, James, Susan Lund, Michael Chui, Jacques Bughin, Jonathan Woetzel, Parul Batra, Ryan Ko, and Saurabh Sanghvi. "Jobs Lost,
Jobs Gained," December 2017. https://www.mckinsey.com/global-
themes/future-of-organizations-and-work/what-the-future-of-work-will-
mean-for-jobs-skills-and-wages.

New technologies will create new jobs, and the skill sets most in demand will evolve as automation and artificial intelligence take on new roles within industries. Job trends can also be viewed as opportunities for self-employment. Where there is demand, there will be business opportunities.

Constant learning, whether on the job or as a freelancer, will become the best safeguard against economic insecurity.

Beyond the economics and opportunities of self-employment lie the less quantifiable but still very real benefits of creating your own business. The wealth experienced by Independent Lifers goes far beyond that which can be tallied on an accounting spreadsheet, as we will see in Chapter 9, The Payoff from an Independent Life.

CHAPTER 9

THE PAYOFF FROM AN INDEPENDENT LIFE

"The only thing worse than starting something and failing... is not starting something."

-Seth Godin, American author and former dot com business executive[128]

So what happened immediately after I quit my job as a teacher and began freelancing? I was not immediately working full-time, yet my income was almost equivalent to what I had been earning as a teacher.

[128] Meah, Asad. 2017. "60 Inspirational Seth Godin Quotes On Success." AwakenTheGreatnessWithin (blog). October 23, 2017. http://awakenthegreatnesswithin.com/60-inspirational-seth-godin-quotes-on-success/.

My level of stress plummeted. My energy level suddenly perked up, and I began using my free time to exercise once again. I took up dancing—a beloved activity from my past—and in the course of one summer, lost those 20 extra pounds I had gained over five years as a teacher.

I was able to quit taking antidepressants, and my outlook on life improved exponentially. I can only imagine the physical improvements to my health that occurred internally.

In short, I found happiness again.

I credit all of these changes to my new-found freedom and the elimination of a huge source of stress (my former job).

Here are the kinds of changes that most of us in business for ourselves expect and experience after making the switch.[129]

- More money
- Less stress
- More work/life balance
- More career certainty
- Better health

---

[129] Upwork, Freelancers Union. "Freelancing in America: 2017 Survey - Upwork." Upwork, October 27, 2017. https://www.upwork.com/i/freelancing-in-america/2017/.

At the same time, freelancers also expect to work harder. In my own case, I worked hard to learn new skills. With each opportunity to work for a new client, I put in hours far beyond those for which I was being paid. This was essential to master skills and online tools new to me that were necessary to create the best possible products for my clients.

Yet, in comparing how hard I was working as a teacher to my efforts as a freelancer, I have to say it felt like the difference between walking with my feet encased in blocks of cement compared to gliding effortlessly through water. I was in my element and loving what I did.

Freedom, interest, responsibility, pride

What can you realistically expect if you go into business for yourself? You can expect all of the benefits cited by freelancers above, and you can also expect to work harder. You can expect to learn news skills and constantly update them. In fact freelancers are proactively preparing for the Fourth Industrial Revolution, "with almost twice as many having participated in skills-related education in the past six months compared to non-freelancers."[130]

---

[130] Upwork, Freelancers Union. "Freelancing in America: 2017 Survey - Upwork." Upwork, October 27, 2017. https://www.upwork.com/i/freelancing-in-america/2017/.

You can expect that your income flow will be more uneven than that of a regular job, and therefore you will need to make a habit of building a savings cushion. In fact, more than half of self-employed prepare by learning new skills and saving money or paying down debt.[131]

"About every quarter, I have a professional crisis," laughs Ivan the Cinematographer. "That is the nature of freelancing, work is very uneven. When work is not good, sometimes I can't see where I'll be in five years time. But my wife says I couldn't stand a regular job for a week!" Most of the pressure that Ivan feels comes from himself. "If I'm not making money, I know it's only my fault."

In terms of pay, that will depend on you: your skills, your industry, your effort, the opportunities that come your way, and probably a bit of luck. People in business for themselves working full-time in 2017 reported the following range of incomes:[132]

- Less than 20% with incomes less than $20,000

---

[131] Upwork, Freelancers Union. "Freelancing in America: 2017 Survey - Upwork." Upwork, October 27, 2017.
https://www.upwork.com/i/freelancing-in-america/2017/
[132] Freshbooks. "New FreshBooks Report Reveals Millennials as Catalysts Behind Self-Employment Movement, Opting for More Autonomy | FreshBooks." Freshbooks, February 21, 2018.
https://www.freshbooks.com/press/releases/new-freshbooks-report-reveals-millennials-as-catalysts-behind-self-employment-movement-opting-for-more-autonomy.

- 21% with incomes ranging from $21,000 to $50,000
- 27% with incomes from $51,000 to $100,000
- 32% with incomes >$101,000.

Additional reasons that people are increasingly choosing to work for themselves (rather than being forced by circumstance) include being your own boss, the ability to choose when and where you work (in many cases), and what projects or clients you will take on. Another plus is that perceptions of freelance workers are becoming more positive.

Of all the benefits associated with the Independent Life, the best one is overall job satisfaction. Self-employed people report job satisfaction at a level 10 percent higher than the traditionally employed. That is probably why, once they begin working for themselves, 97 percent report that they have no intention of ever returning to traditional work.[133]

This job satisfaction stems from not only being your "own boss," but from the ability to more fully realize your potential in the world: to orient toward goals you can be passionate about and stretch yourself to more fully realize your own potential as a human being.

---

[133] Moulton, Cary, and Dave Cosgrave. "Second Annual Self-Employment Report." Freshbooks cloud accounting, February 21, 2018. https://www.freshbooks.com/_themes/freshbooks/brand-assets/2018selfemploymentreport.pdf

Nigel the Tour Leader points out that "work" is defined as something you get paid to do, something you wouldn't do otherwise. Yet much of what he is paid to do does not even feel like work. He's currently contracted to do several books, a couple of which he would want to write anyway, regardless whether he got paid.

Corey the Financial Services Professional represents an array of insurance and banking companies without an affiliation with any single company. "My guiding philosophy is that I want to be able to exercise my skill set to the best of my ability to help people. I have a stewardship mindset where I don't like waste. I'm willing to sacrifice income for myself if the decision or service is not in the long-term interest of my client. That's why my clients like me. I tell it like it is."

The best part of working for yourself? Job satisfaction grows with age![134] That has certainly been the case for me, and I hope it will be the same for you too.

---

[134] Moulton, Cary, and Dave Cosgrave. "Second Annual Self-Employment Report." Freshbooks cloud accounting, February 21, 2018. https://www.freshbooks.com/_themes/freshbooks/brand-assets/2018selfemploymentreport.pdf.

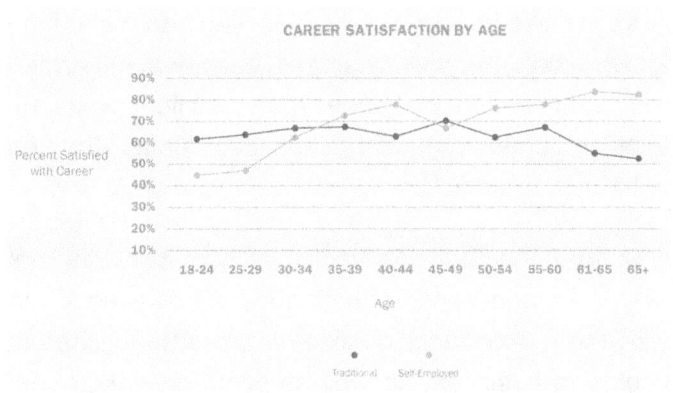

CAREER SATISFACTION BY AGE

Reprinted with permission from *FreshBooks Second Annual Report*, February 21, 2018.

Not for everyone

Working for yourself is not for everyone, and certainly there will continue to be great jobs and wonderful careers in the traditional workplace.

Melanie, the Sport Fishing Entrepreneur provides this admonition about who should work for themselves: "You have to be self-directed. You have to be able to get up and do it on your own with nobody standing over you. If you're an iconoclast or rebellious and can do the work, it's perfect. If you like to problem solve and figure things out, it's perfect.

"But if you'd rather have others tell you to do x, y, and z and then punch out at 5pm, don't think about working for yourself. You don't want to start a business. It's like having a child. Yes, you can make time for yourself, but the business becomes integrated with your life. In the early years, I might wake up thinking about work, work all day, eat dinner, then go right back to work."

It is my hope that this book has helped clarify, not only the mega-trends affecting the way we work, but also the foundational qualities it takes to succeed in your own business, as well as some critical life lessons shared by those who are already living an Independent Life.

Signs pointing you toward being your own boss

You may be an entrepreneur in the embryonic stages if:

- You have recently lost a job and are not looking forward to returning to your industry.
- You are someone who has always wondered what it might be like to run your own business.
- You have an idea for something new that inhabits your brain and won't move out.
- You have a passion for some cause or solution or creation that can't be expressed through your current job.

- You are a self-starter and want or need the flexibility to work from home.
- You are a go-getter with many ideas that you would like to bring to the world.
- You are a free spirit with a ton of motivation to pursue your own path.
- You hate your job or feel too complacent and find yourself thinking there must be more to life than this 9-to-5 drudgery.

Do you fit any of those categories? Are you ready to take the next step on your journey toward an Independent Life? You've already taken an important step by reading this book. Next, you might want to have some conversations with people you know who already work for themselves. Get their stories. Get the full stories behind the ten Independent Lifers I interviewed for this book (at kgreggelliott.com). Don't forget to consult your family as well.

If you know your passion—great!—you can start researching how to turn it into a business. Remember that the hybrid entrepreneurship model says your chances for success are about 30 percent greater if you start part-time.[135] It's wise to begin by figuring out how to work at your business or develop business-related skills part-time before you quit your day job. Writing a business plan is also a recommended

---

[135] Raffiee, Joseph, and Jie Feng. "Should I Quit My Day Job?: A Hybrid Path to Entrepreneurship." Academy of Management Journal 57, no. 4 (August 1, 2014): 936–63. https://doi.org/10.5465/amj.2012.0522.

step[136], and there are many resources for that available online.

If you haven't yet found your passion, or settled on one, follow the steps outlined in Chapter 5 to do so.

The difference between working for someone else and working for yourself is a little like the difference between a caged bird and one who lives wild and free. A caged bird can usually be certain of its next meal, but it is dependent on the benevolence of its owner to survive.

A wild bird, on the other hand, has to bust its tail feathers everyday to get ahead, but when it is successful at surviving, it thrives. It sings all summer long and fills the air with song.

I hope that this book has helped you to weigh the benefits and the limitations of working for others versus the freedom, scary responsibility, joy, and exhilaration of working for yourself. Yes, it does take courage to go into business for yourself, but for 97 out of 100 of us who does so, it's worth it.

To create a job or get a job, that is the question.

In today's rapidly changing world, job turmoil is virtually certain to increase, while trends in the workplace

---

[136] Investopedia Staff. "Top 6 Reasons New Businesses Fail." Investopedia, October 29, 2010. https://www.investopedia.com/slideshow/top-6-reasons-new-businesses-fail/.

combined with a variety of online tools and services are making it easier than ever to go into business for yourself. Odds are that with a few key qualities, a great deal of hard work and determination, and maybe just a little luck, creating a job for yourself is the answer.

PLEASE CONSIDER LEAVING A REVIEW

If you found this book to be valuable or if you obtained helpful insights or if you find yourself now considering important questions that will help you prepare for self-employment, I would really appreciate your quick review on Amazon to tell people how the book helped you. Your review and recommendations for this book will help others to find this message, and maybe, just maybe, to find their way to an Independent Life.

Also, please get in touch! I value above all hearing your stories too! I really want to know if my story and those of the Independent Lifers I interviewed have helped others to better navigate toward their own brand of independence.

Email me at gregg@kgreggelliott.com.

ABOUT THE AUTHOR

Gregg Elliott never aspired to a business of her own, but has been a successful solopreneur since 2009 when she launched K Gregg Consulting. Her niche is to provide communications in support of biodiversity, working lands, climate change adaptation, habitat and wildlife management, conservation science, and green programs for a variety of nonprofits and agencies.

Much to her mingled pride and astonishment, Gregg's business and communications expertise have grown in tandem since establishing K Gregg Consulting. Going independent has given her so much flexibility to organize her day, such great joy in her work, and so many opportunities to meet and collaborate with great people and organizations that she thought if there is a chance others could benefit from her experience, she needed to share it.

When she's not working, she's hiking with the dog, traveling with her daughter, or dancing. Follow Gregg on Twitter (@kgeconservation), or visit her author site at https://www.kgreggelliott.com/.

BIBLIOGRAPHY

Abraham, Stephan. "Layoffs And The Stock Market." Investopedia, January 2, 2013. https://www.investopedia.com/stock-analysis/2013/layoffs-and-the-stock-market-c-hpq0123.aspx.

Accenture. "Artificial Intelligence | Accenture." Accessed March 26, 2018. https://www.accenture.com/us-en/artificial-intelligence-index.

———. "Technology Vision 2017." Accenture LLP. Accessed March 18, 2018. https://www.accenture.com/t20170321T032507__w__/us-en/_acnmedia/Accenture/next-gen-4/tech-vision-2017/pdf/Accenture-TV17-Full.pdf.

Airbnb, Inc. "What Are Airbnb Service Fees? | Airbnb Help Center." Airbnb, Inc. Accessed March 28, 2018. https://www.airbnb.com/help/article/1857/what-are-airbnb-service-fees.

Allen, David. 2002. Getting Things Done: The Art of Stress-Free Productivity: David Allen: 9780142000281: Amazon.Com: Books. Penguin Books.

Balakrishnana, Anita. 2017. "Goldman Sachs Analysis of Autonomous Vehicle Job Loss." CNBC.com. May 22, 2017. https://www.cnbc.com/2017/05/22/goldman-sachs-analysis-of-autonomous-vehicle-job-loss.html.

Bank of America. "U.S. Trust Study Finds Entrepreneurs Choose Career Path of Most Resistance | Bank of America Newsroom," May 23, 2016. http://newsroom.bankofamerica.com/press-releases/global-wealth-and-investment-management/us-trust-study-finds-entrepreneurs-choose-car.

Beane, Matt. "Young Doctors Struggle to Learn Robotic Surgery – so They Are Practicing in the Shadows." *The Conversation*. Accessed March 26, 2018. http://theconversation.com/young-doctors-struggle-to-learn-robotic-surgery-so-they-are-practicing-in-the-shadows-89646.

Blevins, Jason. "Outdoor Industry Will Be Added to the Calculus of the Nation's Gross Domestic Product." The Denver Post, November 29, 2016. https://www.denverpost.com/2016/11/29/outdoor-industry-gross-domestic-product/,

Bluemner, Adam. "How Does the Government Define 'Small Business'?" Software Connect, February 19, 2014. https://softwareconnect.com/blog/how-does-the-government-define-small-business/.

Bolt, Chandler. How to Punch Worry in the Face with Mitch Matthews. Self-Publishing School Podcast. Accessed April 18, 2018. https://self-publishingschool.com/sps-020-punch-worry-face-mitch-matthews/.

Bolt, Seth, and Chandler Bolt. 2014. *Breaking Out Of A Broken System.*

Brown, Jr., H. Jackson. 1991. P.S. I Love You: When Mom Wrote, She Always Saved the Best for Last. Rutledge Hill Pr.

Carnevale, Anthony, Jeff Strohl, Ban Cheah, and Neil Ridley. "Good Jobs Data." Georgetown University Center on Education and the Workforce, 2017. https://goodjobsdata.org/wp-content/uploads/Good-Jobs-wo-BA-final.pdf.

Carson, Johnny. 2018. "Johnny Carson Quotes." BrainyQuote.Com. 2018. https://www.brainyquote.com/quotes/johnny_carson_393392.

Case, Nicky. "How To Become A Centaur." *Journal of Design and Science*, February 6, 2018. https://jods.mitpress.mit.edu/pub/issue3-case.

Clerck, J.-P. De. "Digitization, Digitalization and Digital Transformation: The Differences." i-SCOOP, July 25, 2016. https://www.i-scoop.eu/digitization-digitalization-digital-transformation-disruption/.

Clifford, Catherine. "9 Mind-Blowing Things Elon Musk Said about Robots and AI in 2017," December 18, 2017.

https://www.cnbc.com/2017/12/18/9-mind-blowing-things-elon-musk-said-about-robots-and-ai-in-2017.html.

Conway Center for Family Business. "Family Business Facts." Conway Center for Family Business, 2017. http://www.familybusinesscenter.com/resources/family-business-facts/.

Dawson, Gloria. 2013. "Lettuce Bot: Roomba for Weeds." Modern-farmer.com. Modern Farmer (blog). May 16, 2013. https://modernfarmer.com/2013/05/lettuce-bot-roomba-for-weeds/.

Dickey, Megan Rose. "How Much You Earn As An Uber Driver - Business Insider." *Business Insider*, June 28, 2014. http://www.businessinsider.com/how-much-you-earn-as-an-uber-driver-2014-6.

Doyle, Alison. "How Often Do People Change Jobs?" The Balance. Accessed March 19, 2018. https://www.thebalance.com/how-often-do-people-change-jobs-2060467.

Filippi, Primavera De. "What Blockchain Means for the Sharing Economy." Harvard Business Review, March 15, 2017. https://hbr.org/2017/03/what-blockchain-means-for-the-sharing-economy.

FreshBooks. "New FreshBooks Report Reveals Millennials as Catalysts Behind Self-Employment Movement, Opting for More Autonomy | FreshBooks." FreshBooks, February 21, 2018. https://www.freshbooks.com/press/releases/new-freshbooks-report-reveals-millennials-as-catalysts-behind-self-employment-movement-opting-for-more-autonomy

Goodreads. n.d. "Glenn Carter Quotes (Author of Secrets of the Sharing Economy) | Goodreads." Accessed April 20, 2018. https://www.goodreads.com/author/quotes/14144978.Glenn_Carter.

Graefe, Andreas. "How Algorithms and Human Journalists Will Need to Work Together." The Conversation. Accessed March 18, 2018. http://theconversation.com/how-algorithms-and-human-journalists-will-need-to-work-together-81869.

Hawking, Stephen. "This Is the Most Dangerous Time for Our Planet | Stephen Hawking | Opinion | The Guardian." *The Guardian*, De-

cember 1, 2016.
https://www.theguardian.com/commentisfree/2016/dec/01/stephen
-hawking-dangerous-time-planet-inequality.

Heller, Nathan. "Is the Gig Economy Working?" *The New Yorker*,
May 8, 2017. https://www.newyorker.com/magazine/2017/05/15/is-
the-gig-economy-working.

Hipple, Steven F., and Laurel A. Hammond. "Self-Employment in the
United States : Spotlight on Statistics: U.S. Bureau of Labor Statistics." Accessed April 11, 2018.
https://www.bls.gov/spotlight/2016/self-employment-in-the-united-
states/home.htm.

Hughes, Chris. 2016. "10 Inspirational Gary Vaynerchuk Quotes."
Chris Hughes (blog). September 2, 2016.
https://medium.com/@whosChrisHughes/10-inspirational-gary-
vaynerchuk-quotes-6ac9113e7c11.

Ignaczak, Nina Misuraca. "3 Platforms to Start Your Own Sharing
Service." Shareable, April 22, 2014.
https://www.shareable.net/blog/3-platforms-to-start-your-own-
sharing-service.

Investopedia Staff. "Top 6 Reasons New Businesses Fail." Investopedia, October 29, 2010. https://www.investopedia.com/slide-
show/top-6-reasons-new-businesses-fail/.

Kirkland, Rik. "Competing in the AI Economy: An Interview with MIT's
Andrew McAfee | McKinsey & Company." McKinsey & Company,
March 2018. https://www.mckinsey.com/business-
functions/mckinsey-analytics/our-insights/competing-in-the-ai-
economy-an-interview-with-mits-andrew-mcafee.

Kitroeff, Natalie. "Where Internet Orders Mean Real Jobs, and New
Life for Communities." *The New York Times*, October 22, 2017,
sec. Economy.
https://www.nytimes.com/2017/10/22/business/economy/warehous
e-jobs.html.

Kotler, Steven. "The Passion Recipe: Four Steps To Total Fulfillment." *Forbes*, March 27, 2015.
https://www.forbes.com/sites/stevenkotler/2015/03/27/the-passion-
recipe-four-steps-to-total-fulfillment/.

Lund, Susan. "What the Rise of the Freelance Economy Means for the Future of Work." *Huffington Post*, October 30, 2015. https://www.huffingtonpost.com/susan-lund/freelance-economy-future-work_b_8420866.html.

Manyika, James, Susan Lund, Michael Chui, Jacques Bughin, Jonathan Woetzel, Parul Batra, Ryan Ko, and Saurabh Sanghvi. "Jobs Lost, Jobs Gained," December 2017. https://www.mckinsey.com/global-themes/future-of-organizations-and-work/what-the-future-of-work-will-mean-for-jobs-skills-and-wages.

Marx, Karl, and Friedrich Engels. 1848. The Communist Manifesto. 12th Media Services. https://www.amazon.com/Communist-Manifesto-Karl-Marx/dp/1680922106/ref=tmm_hrd_swatch_0?_encoding=UTF8&qid=&sr=.

Mather, Mark. "Fact Sheet: Aging in the United States – Population Reference Bureau." Population Reference Bureau, January 13, 2016. https://www.prb.org/aging-unitedstates-fact-sheet/.

Matofska, Benita. "What Is the Sharing Economy?" the people who share, 2016. http://www.thepeoplewhoshare.com/blog/what-is-the-sharing-economy/.

Matthews, Mitch. 2018. *Dream Job: Redefined: The New Rules for Creating a Career That Matters and Doing Work You Love*. MMJM Companies, Incorporated.

Mazur, Michal. 2016. "Six Ways Drones Are Revolutionizing Agriculture." MIT Technology Review, July 20, 2016. https://www.technologyreview.com/s/601935/six-ways-drones-are-revolutionizing-agriculture/.

Meah, Asad. 2017. "60 Inspirational Seth Godin Quotes On Success." AwakenTheGreatnessWithin (blog). October 23, 2017. http://awakenthegreatnesswithin.com/60-inspirational-seth-godin-quotes-on-success/ .

Mishel, Lawrence, Elise Gould, and Josh Bivens. "Wage Stagnation in Nine Charts." *Economic Policy Institute* (blog), January 6, 2015. https://www.epi.org/publication/charting-wage-stagnation/.

Monocle. "The Social Impact Entrepreneurs Making A Difference - UNLIMITED by UBS," November 9, 2016. https://www.unlimited.world/monocle/when-does-making-a-difference-mean-more-than-money.

Moore, George. 2018. "A Quote by George Moore." Goodreads.Com. 2018. https://www.goodreads.com/quotes/897172-a-winner-is-just-a-loser-who-tried-one-more.

Moulton, Cary, and Dave Cosgrave. "Second Annual Self-Employment Report." FreshBooks cloud accounting, February 21, 2018. https://www.freshbooks.com/_themes/freshbooks/brand-assets/2018selfemploymentreport.pdf.

Muro, Mark, and Sifan Liu On 11/27/17 at 11:31 AM. 2017. "The US Is Digitalizing at Warp Speed. What Could Possibly Go Wrong?" Newsweek, November 27, 2017. http://www.newsweek.com/us-digitalizing-warp-speed-what-could-possibly-go-wrong-723240.

Muro, Mark, Sifan Liu, Jacob Whiton, and Siddharth Kulkarni. "Digitalization and the American Workforce." The Brookings Institution, November 2017. https://www.brookings.edu/research/digitalization-and-the-american-workforce/.

Nir, Sarah Maslin. "Be Nice — You Won't Finish Last." *The New York Times*, April 7, 2017, sec. Education Life. https://www.nytimes.com/2017/04/07/education/edlife/be-nice-you-wont-finish-last.html.

O'Donovan, Caroline, and Jeremy Singer-Vine. "How Much Uber Drivers Actually Make Per Hour." BuzzFeed, June 22, 2016. https://www.buzzfeed.com/carolineodonovan/internal-uber-driver-pay-numbers.

Oliver, Mary. *New and Selected Poems*. Boston, MA: Beacon Press, 1992.

OpenAI. "OpenAI Charter." OpenAI Blog, April 9, 2018. https://blog.openai.com/openai-charter/.

Outdoor Industry Association. "The Outdoor Recreation Economy." Outdoor Industry Association, 2017. https://outdoorindustry.org/advocacy/.

Puzzanghera, Jim. "One-Fifth of U.S. Workers Were Laid off in Past Five Years, Study Says." *Los Angeles Times.* September 24, 2014, sec. Business. http://www.latimes.com/business/la-fi-layoffs-unemployment-jobs-economy-20140924-story.html.

Raffiee, Joseph, and Jie Feng. "Should I Quit My Day Job?: A Hybrid Path to Entrepreneurship." *Academy of Management Journal* 57, no. 4 (August 1, 2014): 936–63. https://doi.org/10.5465/amj.2012.0522.

Rideshare Dashboard. 2014. "Can Lyft or Uber Drivers Claim Unemployment?" Rideshare Dashboard (blog). December 25, 2014. https://medium.com/@RideshareDash/can-lyft-or-uber-drivers-claim-unemployment-e67efa688b89.

Ridester Staff. "Uber Fees: How Much Does Uber ACTUALLY Take From Drivers?" Ridester. Accessed March 18, 2018. https://www.ridester.com/uber-fees/.

Seth, Shobhit. "Entrepreneurs and Entrepreneurship Defined." Investopedia, September 25, 2014. https://www.investopedia.com/articles/investing/092514/entrepreneur-vs-small-business-owner-defined.asp.

Shea, Christopher. "Nobelist Muhammad Yunus: Be A Go-Getter, Not A Job Getter." *NPR.Org* (blog). Accessed March 18, 2018. https://www.npr.org/sections/goatsandsoda/2014/09/23/350640122/nobelist-muhammad-yunus-be-a-go-getter-not-a-job-getter.

Smith, N. Craig. "Who's Responsible? The Ethics of the Sharing Economy | Alliance for Research on Corporate Sustainability." Alliance for Research on Corporate Sustainability. Accessed March 18, 2018. https://corporate-sustainability.org/whos-responsible-the-ethics-of-the-sharing-economy/.

Standing, Guy. "Meet the Precariat, the New Global Class Fueling the Rise of Populism." World Economic Forum, November 9, 2016. https://www.weforum.org/agenda/2016/11/precariat-global-class-rise-of-populism/.

Stephens, Dale J. "Do You Really Have to Go to College?" New York Times. *The Choice Blog* (blog), March 7, 2013. https://thechoice.blogs.nytimes.com/2013/03/07/do-you-really-have-to-go-to-college/.

Szoldra, Paul. "Elon Musk Thinks Sci-Fi Nightmare Scenarios About Artificial Intelligence Could Really Happen." *Business Insider*, October 24, 2014. http://www.businessinsider.com/elon-musk-artificial-intelligence-mit-2014-10.

TaskRabbit, Inc. "What Is the TaskRabbit Service Fee?" TaskRabbit Support. Accessed March 28, 2018. http://support.taskrabbit.com/hc/en-us/articles/204411610-What-is-the-TaskRabbit-Service-Fee-.

Tesolin, Arupa. "12 Power Thoughts for Creators Everywhere | LinkedIn." LinkedIn, April 17, 2014. https://www.linkedin.com/pulse/20140417164905-4785314-12-rules-for-a-heroes-destiny/.

———. "Work Is Broken - This Is Jobageddon | LinkedIn," August 1, 2014. https://www.linkedin.com/pulse/20140801141146-4785314-job-sharknado-looming/.

Torpey, Elka, and Andrew Hogan. "Working in a Gig Economy : Career Outlook: U.S. Bureau of Labor Statistics." Bureau of Labor Statistics. Career Outlook (blog), May 2016. https://www.bls.gov/careeroutlook/2016/article/what-is-the-gig-economy.htm.

U.S. Census. n.d. "Nonemployer Definitions." United States Census. Accessed March 28, 2018. https://www.census.gov/epcd/nonemployer/view/define.html.

U.S. Department of Commerce, B. E. A. "Bureau of Economic Analysis." Bureau of Economic Analysis, February 14, 2018. https://www.bea.gov/newsreleases/industry/orsa/orsanewsrelease.htm.

Uber. "Legal | Uber." United States. Uber, 2018. https://www.uber.com/legal/terms/us/.

Upwork, Freelancers Union. "Freelancing in America: 2017 Survey - Upwork." Upwork, October 27, 2017. https://www.upwork.com/i/freelancing-in-america/2017/.

Vilorio, Dennis. "Self-Employment: What to Know to Be Your Own Boss : Career Outlook: U.S. Bureau of Labor Statistics." United States Bureau of Labor Statistics. Accessed March 28, 2018.

https://www.bls.gov/careeroutlook/2014/article/self-employment-what-to-know-to-be-your-own-boss.htm.

Wartzman, Rick. *The End of Loyalty, the Rise and Fall of Good Jobs in America.* New York: Public Affairs, 2017.

World Economic Forum. "The Future of Jobs." World Economic Forum, January 2016.
http://www3.weforum.org/docs/WEF_Future_of_Jobs.pdf.

Yunus, Muhammad. *A World of Three Zeroes.* Melbourne | London: Scribe Publications, 2017.

Zwick, Steve. "Ten Things You Need To Know About The Restoration Economy." *Ecosystem Marketplace* (blog). Accessed March 18, 2018. https://www.forest-trends.org/ecosystem_marketplace/ten-things-need-know-restoration-economy/.

www.ingramcontent.com/pod-product-compliance
Lightning Source LLC
Chambersburg PA
CBHW051906170526
45168CB00001B/260